Collecting Authentic Indian Arts and Crafts

Traditional Work of the Southwest

Indian Arts and Crafts Association
&
Council for Indigenous
Arts and Culture

Book Publishing Company
Summertown, Tennessee

Copyright 1999 by Indian Arts and Crafts Association and Council for Indigenous Arts and Culture

Cover design by Studio Haus
Book design by Jerry Lee Hutchens

Book Publishing Company
P. O. Box 99
Summertown, TN 38483

03 02 01 00 99   6 5 4 3 2 1

ISBN 1-57067-062-5

Collecting authentic Indian arts and crafts, Traditional work of the Southwest / Indian Arts and
        Crafts Association & Council for Indigenous Arts and Culture
                        p. cm.
                Includes bibliographical references.
                ISBN 1-57067-062-5 (alk. paper)
        1. Indian art--Collectors and collecting--North America.
        2. Indians of North America--Antiquities--Collectors and collecting.
        3. Indians of North America--Material culture--Collectors and collecting. I. Indian Arts
        & Crafts Association (U.S.) II. Council for Indigenous Arts and Culture.
        E98.A7C553 1999   99-19848
        704.03'97'0075--dc21   CIP
                                                                Rev.

PROTECT AND PROMOTE
NATIVE AMERICAN ART & CRAFTS
THROUGH EDUCATION.

Table of Contents

Acknowledgements   5

Introduction   6

Jewelry   7

    Technical Aspects   10

    The Old and New   22

    Additional Resources   24

    A Jeweler's Story   25

Pueblo Pottery   27

    Making Traditional Pottery   27

    Non-Handcrafted or Commercial Pottery   31

    Additional Resources   39

    A Hopi-Tewa Potter   41

Navajo Rugs   43

    Origin   44

    Weaving   46

    Imitations   48

    Tips for Collecting   51

    Additional Resources   52

    A Navajo Weaver   53

Baskets   55

    Origin   55

    Making a Basket   57

    Identifying   65

    Collecting and Care   68

    Additional Resources   72

    A Navajo Basket Weaver   73

Fetish Carvings 75

Origin 76

Carving 78

Imitation Is Not Always Flattery 80

Identifying 82

Additional Resources 82

A Fetish Carver 83

An Artist Looks at Fetishes 85

Katsina Dolls 89

Origin 91

Carving 93

Authenticity 94

Collecting 96

Additional Resources 98

A Traditional Hopi Carver 99

Collecting Authentic Arts and Crafts 103

Tips 104

Common Questions 107

Protection Laws 109

Recommended General Reading 119

Photography Credits 120

Index 121

Acknowledgements

This book is a collaborative effort by dedicated members of the Indian Arts and Crafts Association (IACA) and the Council for Indigenous Arts and Culture (CIAC). A unique team of American Indian artists and art dealers came together to write this guide to collecting contemporary Indian art. We wish to give special thanks to **Pam Phillips**, owner of Skystone N' Silver in Hobart, IN, for her contributions in the jewelry, beadwork, and quillwork sections. **Charles King**, owner of King Galleries in Scottsdale, AZ, is responsible for the section on pottery. **Georgiana Kennedy Simpson**, owner of Kennedy Gallery in Albuquerque, NM, and Kennedy Indian Arts in Bluff, UT, put together the sections on rugs, baskets, fetishes, and katsina dolls. The section "Tips on Collecting Native American Arts and Crafts" was created by **Susan Pourian** of The Indian Craft Shop in Washington, DC. Finally, **Andy Abeita**, an Isleta Pueblo sculptor, is responsible for the section "American Indian Arts and Crafts Protection Law." A special thanks goes to **Kent McManis** and **Robert Jeffries** of Grey Dog Trading in Tucson, AZ, and **Tony Eriacho** of Eriacho Indian Arts in Zuni, NM. Their knowledge, guidance, and expertise was essential in various sections of this book.

The heart and soul of this book lies with the individual artists who were generous with their time and knowledge in sharing their personal viewpoints. Each artist is a shining example of the individual vision, patience, and talent which makes contemporary Native American art so dynamic and beautiful.

Due to a generous arrangement with the Book Publishing Company of Summertown, Tennessee, proceeds from this book will benefit the Indian Arts and Crafts Association and Council for Indigenous Arts and Culture.

The Indian Arts and Crafts Association is a not-for-profit organization which was formed in 1974. Its mission is to support the effective protection and ethical promotion of authentic Native American art and material culture.

In 1998, the Council for Indigenous Arts and Culture was formed with these principal goals in mind: a) to increase public awareness and appreciation for the preservation of the culture, arts, and history of North American Indians, and b) to provide North American Indian communities, through education and research, tools to develop and strengthen the economic foundation of their arts and crafts. The money raised by this book is earmarked for additional educational programs promoting the unique beauty of authentic Indian art.

We wish to thank Sandy Hummingbird for her efforts in editing this edition. Finally, the entire project would have been impossible without the patient prodding of Jerry Lee Hutchens, editor for the Book Publishing Company. The insanity of bringing together so many authors on one project was handled with skill and humor by Jerry.

Introduction

In 1974, the Indian Arts and Crafts Association was created to promote, preserve, and protect authentic Indian art. Today, over 700 artists, dealers, museums, and collector members of the association, work to represent handmade Native American and Canadian Indian art to the world. The Council for Indigenous Arts and Culture was founded in 1998 as an independent organization dedicated to documenting the social and economic import of Native American arts on artists, their families, and their communities. Providing technical assistance to tribes and law enforcement agencies to protect the arts is a primary goal as well. Education and information are the key elements to success. Together, the two organizations are working diligently to further the causes of American and Canadian Indian artists and protect artists, art dealers, and consumers from fraudulent business practices mushrooming throughout the industry due to the popularity of American Indian art and culture.

This book started as a consumer-tip brochure. Discussions made us quickly realize our "brochure" was transforming into a book. The collaborators bring decades of experience and individual research to this project. Each involved individual felt this educational tool to be of such importance as to donate their time to the effort. The result is a detailed volume on collecting contemporary Indian art which benefits collectors and dealers while providing necessary revenues for future educational projects.

This book contains not only the history and process of the art, but solid suggestions to help you become a better collector. We also wanted to provide individual artist perspectives so you can look at the artwork from their viewpoint. Remember, knowledge is power! Knowing that no single volume can contain every bit of information you need, at the end of each chapter and at the end of the book, we suggest additional readings. The books suggested have been reviewed for quality of content and usefulness. Finally, if you have had purchases misrepresented to you, we give guidelines on how to resolve the problem. We think, however, if you follow our guidelines for collecting, you will hopefully avoid the problem of buying misrepresented artwork.

With the Indian Arts and Crafts Association celebrating its 25th Anniversary in 1999, we feel this book is a fitting culmination of many years of effort by members of the association to further knowledge on authentic Indian arts and crafts.

For further information about the Indian Arts and Crafts Association, call 505-265-9149 or write us at the following address:

INDIAN ARTS AND CRAFTS ASSOCIATION
122 La Veta, NE, Suite B
Albuquerque, NM 87108

You may also visit us via the Internet at www.iaca.com.
The e-mail address is iaca@ix.netcom.com.

Jewelry

Pam Phillips

Is it adornment? Security? A medium of trade? Is it practical or is it art?

Jewelry is all of these things. Jewelry has always been a part of people's lives. It designates status, achievement, and a desire to be noticed. Whether it's a necklace made of strung teeth from a prehistoric cave bear or a strand of diamonds around the throat of an Academy Award winner, jewelry has always been an important part of life.

As soon as people were able to meet the basic needs of life—shelter, food, clothing, making tools and weapons—their attention turned to making items of beauty and the arts were formed. In the few moments of free time, creativity surfaced. Colorful seeds were strung on fiber or sinew; pots were decorated by painting them with dyes made from plants and minerals. Baskets were woven not only for necessity, but woven with a pattern that was pleasing. Cave walls and smooth rock faces were carved with petroglyph figures representing the realistic items of daily life or the spiritual and mystical figures of sacred beliefs.

Since early people were nomadic, jewelry was a perfect medium for adornment. It could be worn rather than carried and left the hands free. It was also a negotiable trade item and used as a medium of exchange for necessities. Early jewelry was fashioned from items already formed and found in nature. Bones, feathers, seeds, stones, flakes of mica, shells, and animal teeth were most commonly used. With a minimum amount of time and effort, they could be shaped or strung and used as bracelets, necklaces, earrings, or tied onto belts, pouches, and other items. As civilization progressed, carefully formed beads made of seeds and stone, precisely drilled and strung, were highly sought as trade items. Beadmaking became a full-time occupation for some and jewelry making as a profession was born. Later, as technology progressed, came the use of precious metals and ceramics or glass making. Beautiful beads with intricate patterns and colors were made and traded all over the world. Precious and semi-precious stones such as diamonds, sapphires, rubies, emeralds, lapis lazuli, and turquoise were fashioned into jewelry, designating royalty and power.

The wealth of governments was held in jewelry, as well as the wealth of many individuals. Crowns and scepters encrusted with precious stones were used to identify and denote power.

The Koh-i-Nor diamond of India, found approximately 5,000 years ago, was part of the Royal jewels at Delhi, home of the "Peacock Throne."

Stolen by the Persians around 1739 during their conquest of India, it seemed to bring ill luck, death, and destruction to its new owners. It was recovered by an Indian noble and became part of the Punjab treasury at Lahore until 1849, when the East India Company received it as partial payment for damages sustained during the Sikh revolt. It was presented to Queen Victoria and is now part of the British Crown Jewels.

The Hope Diamond, originally part of an even larger stone, came from India to France as part of the wealth of Louis XIV. It disappeared during the French Revolution (1792) and surfaced years later in London and was subsequently purchased by an American, Thomas Hope. He sold it to a Turkish Sultan who later sold it to New York jeweler, Harry Winston. Winston then donated it to the Smithsonian Museum. Many precious and semi-precious stones and pearls have formed the backbone of wealth among many governments.

Native American jewelry has also played a diverse role in Indian culture. In ancient ruins, jewelry is one of the items that is almost always found. It had an important function in life as well as in death. In many societies, the importance of the person's role during life was characterized by the amount and quality of the jewelry accompanying the body's burial.

At Cahokia Mounds, one burial was accompanied by over 11,000 freshwater pearls. Many were drilled and fashioned into jewelry or sewn onto clothing. Intricately carved and incised shells were also used extensively throughout mound-building societies in Mississippi, Tennessee, Ohio, Indiana, Illinois, Iowa, Wisconsin and Oklahoma.

Shells and corals were traded for turquoise, jet, hematite, and other prized stones. These materials were again traded for items made from such metals as copper and silver. Natural veins of copper and silver, pure enough to be used in their native state without smelting, comprised the metals used in early jewelry making. Later, coins and other trade items made from metals were introduced by the Europeans.

Different techniques and styles developed, as the introduction of European trade items melded with creative designs drawn from the various traditional cultures. As a broad generalization, jewelry created along the coastal areas, where there was walrus or whales, relied heavily on drilled shell and ivory. In woodland areas, animal teeth, porcupine quills, and beaded leather were common. This was true among Plains tribes as well, as many had originated as Woodland tribes or traded extensively with them. In the Southwest, turquoise and other colorful native stones were prized and much time and effort was spent in carefully shaping, drilling, and polishing these materials to enhance their natural beauty.

While jewelry signified wealth and power to the ruling classes, it also was very much the personal expression of individuals as well. Used as personal adornment, it separated the individual from the group. It also allowed a person to trade for commodities and represented a well-known and regular medium of value.

After the establishment of trading posts and reservations, Native Americans depended more on outsiders for their needs, but still used jewelry as a form of storing their wealth. Banks were relatively unknown on the reservation, but they were also unnecessary. Why would people put their trust in money formulated by a government that had repeatedly lied to them? Besides, it was mere paper and had little meaning. Precious and semi-precious stones set in silver or gold or strung in lengths had intrinsic value. Instead of the bank, a more practical repository for jewelry was the trading post.

Very often the trader was a trusted friend. Because of this relationship, the use of pawn developed, and used to the greatest degree in the Southwest. While it is still used today, it was used far more extensively in the past when Native Americans relied heavily on the barter of goods in exchange for the items they needed. If crops hadn't been harvested, sheep sheared, or cattle readied for sale, jewelry would often be left as a promise to return and pay for goods taken. Sometimes unexpected events dictated the purchase of additional food or items needed for ceremonies. Money or commodities would be extended by the trader in return for the jewelry. If the agreed upon interest was received on a regular basis, the item would continue to be held by the trader. If the person redeemed the debt, the jewelry was then returned.

This provided the loan system that would otherwise have been provided by a bank. Sometimes an item was pawned merely for safekeeping, much as a bank will provide a safety deposit box for an agreed-upon fee. Some jewelry and other items were used only for specific purposes (religious or ceremonial) and thus could be safely stored at the trading post. If a person never made the interest payments or never redeemed the item pawned after a period of time, the trader could sell the item and recoup his cost. Jewelry sold in this manner was usually quite reasonable and often very unique. Since these pieces had been made and worn by Native Americans themselves, they frequently were different or more intricate than pieces made for commercial sale. Collectors realized the value in obtaining jewelry in this fashion and "pawn jewelry" became highly sought after. It was thought to be more desirable as it was frequently heavier and had high-grade stones.

Many times in the market today jewelry is pawned that is of poor quality or because it could not be sold otherwise. Much of what is offered for sale may contain imitation stones or may be mass produced. Many hours may be spent examining average pieces to uncover heavy, old items that were more common in the past. When good examples are found, they are usually priced accordingly. Most of the collectible pieces are sold before the general public ever has the chance to see them. Usually they go into private collections or to gallery owners and are then offered for sale.

Technical Aspects

The different styles of jewelry described in this chapter represent the major lapidary and silversmithing techniques that are used in Indian jewelry, but certainly do not represent all that is being done today. Indian jewelers are among the most creative, innovative, and talented jewelers to be found anywhere in the world. Making the best of what was available, they adapt many materials to their work. Even old phonograph records were used to supply black material when jet was not available or at hand! Traditionally, materials used were turquoise (green or blue), corals (white, pink, or red), spiny oyster (red to orange, sometimes purple), green snail (white mother of pearl), jet (black fossil coal), petrified wood, pipestone (reddish-brown), and ivory. These were commonly available locally or by trade. In contemporary times, any stone available is used. We now frequently see malachite, azurite, sugilite, lapis lazuli, amber, opal, diamonds, sapphires, garnets, pearls, hematite, and virtually any stone that is available, used in traditional and contemporary designs. It is also quite common to see gold used in place of silver.

The use of materials and techniques are limited only by the artist's imagination and creative ability. This brings up an important point. There are technicians and there are artists. Some of the people making jewelry learn one or more techniques and a few designs and make the same pieces over and over. While they are talented at what they do, it is a skill, not an art. Other jewelers use materials like a painter uses paint. They create visually beautiful images of the imagination and rarely repeat the same design. These artists can compete with any jewelers in the world.

Beadwork

Beadwork used in jewelry was usually done on leather. Early beads were made from seeds, bone or stone by drilling a hole through the material and then shaping the outside into a circle or oval. This was done by using a stick of wood or bone with a pointed end attached to a crosspiece with a twisted leather thong. This could be pumped by hand using an abrasive to hasten the process, such as powdered shell or sand. The bead would be drilled halfway through on one side and then turned and drilled from the opposite side. This process would leave a funnel shaped hole, wider on the outside and smaller in the center. The beads could then

Beadwork on leather
 a. Round beaded pin.
 b. Oval beaded buckle.
 c. Beaded flower hair ornament.

be strung and shaped against a hard rough surface to the desired size. By varying the size, shape, and color, innumerable designs could be made. In later times European traders introduced the use of glass beads, ranging from large decorative beads such as Chevrons, to various sizes of pony beads and seed beads.

*Quillwork on leather
a. Hair ornament with dyed and natural quills and a beaded edge.
b. Necklace with a quilled medallion and beaded edge on beaded necklace.*

Quillwork

Quillwork was done as individual pieces of jewelry, such as pendants or earrings and by decorating clothing around a yoke, down a sleeve, or around a cuff. It was a difficult and time-consuming process (and it still is), since a porcupine does not willingly give up its main defense. Picking the quills out by hand is a painful process. The easiest way is to take a piece of thin leather or dense cloth, such as felt, and press the material against the quills opposite the direction in which they are lying. With a quick motion pull the material free and the barbed quills will come out embedded in the material. They can then be picked out and sorted by size. The guard quills are longer on the neck and back. Shorter quills are underneath and form the sides. Since they are hollow, they can be easily sewn but need to be made flexible by soaking and flattening. This can be done using a hand held stick, or by holding the quill between thumb and forefinger and pulling through the teeth (top and bottom clenched together). The quills can then be sewn using their natural color of ivory with a brown end, or dyed to make bright colors such as red, yellow, purple, etc. This complicated art form, also used to decorate baskets, is seen less today than in the past. It is tedious and time consuming but creates an appearance that cannot be achieved in any other way.

Metalsmithing

Except for a relatively small amount of jewelry that was made using silver and copper from almost pure veins, most metal jewelry was not common until the mid-1800s. Mexican silversmiths living along the Rio Grande Valley probably taught some of the Pueblo, as well as the Navajo artists, how to work silver. Mexican and American coins were used until outlawed by the governments, hence the term coin silver.

Coin silver was 85% to 90% silver alloyed with copper. After the use of coins was outlawed, one ounce ingots and sheet silver were supplied. Sterling silver (92.5% silver, 7.5% copper) was commonly used after 1940. Imitation and machine-made Indian look-alike jewelry may use the terms German silver or Denver silver. These items contain no silver at all and are composed of a combination of copper, zinc, and nickel.

There are several techniques commonly used in the metalsmithing art of jewelry making.

Sterling silver hand hammered bracelet by Mark Chee.

Hand hammered, one of the earliest forms of silversmithing, means literally hammering silver by hand into desired shapes on an anvil or other hard, smooth surface. The piece can then be decorated by using a graver (metal hand tool) to incise the surface of the silver to form a border or pattern. Metal carved stamps may be used to hammer the design into the silver. Since hammering the silver causes it to become work-hardened, it then must be annealed (heat treated) to soften it again. Repeated hammering compresses the molecules and makes silver brittle and prone to cracking or breaking. Early silversmiths used a bellows to make a small fire burn very hot so they could anneal the pieces as they were working. They tried to evenly heat the piece without melting it, much as a blacksmith would do when pounding out horseshoes. After the design is finished the edges can be filed and then the piece can be polished using wet leather and an abrasive such as sand or ground stone.

Silver bracelet by Ira Custer, using sandcast technique with no additional stones or decoration.

Sandcast is the ancient form of hand casting jewelry. In this process the design is carved into a flat piece of stone or into sand, along with a channel to pour the melted silver into and several vents for the heated air to escape. A second piece of stone is secured tightly to the first piece and the molten silver is poured from a crucible into the opening. After the metal has cooled and hardened the piece is removed, but it is far from finished! It needs to have the "sprue" shaved off—the part of the mold where the metal has hardened in the channel and not meant to be part of the piece. There may be other pieces also that have started to flow outside the design that need to be shaved. Then all edges need to be filed smooth and the whole piece has to have all surfaces ground and polished. Sandcast designs have a unique look but are not an easy way to form jewelry. While sandstone may have been used for molds in the past, it became quickly apparent that it was not well suited for this purpose. The molten silver would fracture the stone, ruining the design. Tufa stone is most commonly used since it is a volcanic stone, and able to withstand the high temperatures. Coin silver melts at 1,615 degrees and sterling silver melts at 1,640 degrees. Sandcast jewelry is beautiful and simplistic in design, making it easy to wear with a variety of clothing styles. Sometimes turquoise or other stones are added for extra effect.

Repousse means raising a design on the front surface by striking the back surface using a metal or hardwood die and a hammer. This is no easy task since striking too hard may ruin the piece, and striking too softly will

Repousse and stamped bowguard featuring hand fabricated silver with raised design surrounded by stampwork. Buttons on either side domed by hand. Created by Robert Kelley.

not raise the pattern. Also, repeated striking will not only work-harden the piece but will not raise a clear imprint. When creating certain patterns, each element of the design must be raised using the same force. After the work is completed on the backside, the raised pattern on the front may be outlined by graving a channel around it, decorating with stampwork, or texturing a contrasting surface. Details of the stamping or graving may be brought out by oxidizing the background or low spots and polishing the surface or high spots. Silver will normally darken with exposure to light and air over time, but the process can be made permanent by altering the surface of the silver with liver of sulphur or potassium salts. This creates contrast and defines the design.

Applique uses sheet silver as a background. The design elements are then cut out of a lighter gauge of sheet silver and soldered onto the piece. They may be additionally decorated by etching or stampwork.

The various methods of silversmithing described so far—hand hammered, repousse, sandcast, applique, and the use of many different stamps and graved patterns—most commonly describe Navajo style jewelry. While stones may be used to accent or highlight a piece, they are simply cut cabochons or free form pieces. Most of the time and attention is devoted to the metalsmithing. Common elements in Navajo style jewelry are leaves, flowers, scrolls, feathers, and wire used in a variety of complex designs.

Overlay is another style of intricate metalsmithing. Hopi silversmiths Fred Kabotie and Paul Saufkie, working with the Museum of Northern Arizona in Flagstaff, developed this style around 1938. However, due to World War II, this style was not commonly seen until later in the 1940s. Overlay is achieved literally by laying one piece of silver over another. The top sheet of silver has the cut-out design, often very intricate, and it is then sweated to the bottom sheet of silver by heating the two pieces to just under the melting point. It then has the appearance of a single layer. The background is incised with a pattern of fine lines done with a hammer and a fine chisel or nail. Most artists create their own imprint by filing a nail or other piece of hardened steel for this purpose. By striking this piece repeatedly and evenly across the surface of the underlying sheet of silver, a contrasting design is created. Oxidizing this underlying sheet makes the raised polished surface stand out with three-dimensional clarity. Sometimes the top surface is polished with an abrasive such as a steel wheel or steel wool to give it a soft brushed patina rather than the highly reflective polish that is usually seen. Stones are sometimes used to accent the design, but more often the silver work stands alone. This overlay technique makes later Hopi jewelry very identifiable. Prior to the late 1930s, Hopi work looked very much the same as Navajo work.

Lapidary

Techniques described below focus the design of the jewelry on the stone work, or lapidary design, rather than on the silversmithing techniques. In the following styles of jewelry, silver is used merely to form a framework to hold the stones.

Heishi. Though commonly used to describe turquoise, heishi was originally used to describe a technique of making discoidal beads of shell. By cutting shell into small pieces, drilling each piece, and stringing it on a rod or wire and shaping it against a rough surface, uniform beads are made and then strung on a softer material so that they move. When fashioned with care they feel extremely smooth and silky, and will flow with movement. The Santo Domingo Pueblo is known for this style of jewelry, although it has been copied extensively in the Philippines and Taiwan. Many necklaces of this type have been found in ancient ruins such as Chaco Canyon, Mesa Verde and others, as well as from the Mound

Sterling silver Hopi overlay necklace (left) by Lawrance Saufkie. A Heishi necklace made of black oyster shell, white clam shell and pipestone.

Builders in the Midwest and Southeast. Clearly it is a very early jewelry form and is still prized today. This technique is very labor intensive and requires not only skill but patience.

Needlepoint is used to describe a Zuni-style of stonework that is characterized by a small piece of turquoise slightly wider in the middle and pointed at both ends. It is thin and elongated and gives a very delicate appearance. Set in fine silver bezels in rows with drops of silver at the ends, the design is one of delicate beauty. Using a turquoise without matrix is desirable so that the appearance is uniform and perfectly matched.

Petit point is similar to needlepoint though the shape is more oval or tear drop. It is frequently seen in combination with oval or round

Needlepoint necklace and earring set of silver and turquoise crafted by Rudell and Nancy Laconsello.

stones to create a style called clusterwork. In the photo on page 19 the petit point stones are arranged in a circular or oval fashion in several rows around a center stone.

Inlay can be achieved in several ways. One style is mosaic inlay. In this technique, small stones of the same or differing materials are arranged to form a geometric pattern or an actual representation such as a dancer, animal or flowers. Each stone is perfectly fitted to the stone next to it, forming a design that is smooth on the surface with no gaps between the stones. They are held in place by using epoxy and a bezel around the

These are fine examples of petit point clusterwork a red coral bracelet and ring with coral cut in tear drop shape of petit point style and stones clustered in concentric rings around a center stone. Crafted by Alice Quam.

perimeter of the design. In ancient times, inlay was done on top of shells and the pieces were cemented on with pine pitch. While inlay is traditionally thought to be representative of Zuni jewelry, many Navajo jewelers have used this technique for years.

Channel inlay is a technique that uses a silver framework and additional channels or pieces of silver to form the design. The empty spaces are filled with various stones perfectly cut to fill the spaces within the design. In this way, each stone is surrounded by a channel of silver.

This channel inlay bracelet by Robert Henry has 375 individual stones of spiny oyster shell, turquoise, and white mother of pearl. Each piece is surrounded by a silver channel on all sides.

Raised inlay mudhead katsina bolo of red coral, turquoise, jet, green snail shell, and gold lip shell by Bev Etsitty. On the right is a bear claw buckle by Robert Kelley, with turquoise and coral, hand fabricated leaf, flowers and scroll work.

Raised inlay can be done as channel or mosaic or a combination of the two. In this style some of the stones are cut deeper than the surrounding stones so that part of the design is raised above the surface around it. In addition, the raised stones may be carved to simulate a realistic picture, such as details of clothing on a dancer, feathers in the wings of a bird or petals in a flower.

Combination of techniques
Hand fabricated necklace using handmade bezels for each stone and decorating silver with contrasting finish. Part of the finish is stippled and part of the surface is smooth with a high polish. Grooved lines are oxidized to outline and contrast. There are individual cabochons of coral, lapis lazuli, and opal, as well as mosaic inlay on the pendant using the same stones. Created by 1997 Indian Artist of the Year, Michael Kirk.

The Old and the New

Among many Indian peoples, jewelry making is an an art form of long standing tradition. From thousands of years ago until the present time, it has been an expression of beauty and of self. In modern times, jewelry is frequently made for others and the use of new materials and creative designs is encouraged to meet the demand of the marketplace. Until recently, the Indian jewelry market was a narrow piece of the world surrounding the areas where the jewelry was made; remote places where tourists traveled by train and later by car. Now Indian jewelry is collected and appreciated all over the world.

As with many handmade art forms, Indian jewelry making must be recognized and protected in order to survive. In the past, Indian jewelry has cycled with trends. These trends made it fashionable to support indigenous arts, decorate with Indian art, or wear Indian jewelry to indicate a certain mindset. As Indian jewelry has become increasingly desirable, this art form is being copied. It is copied in foreign countries using inferior materials and underpaid workers. It is copied by machines and non-Indian people and sold as Indian handmade. There are laws to protect Indian arts, but most consumers are not aware of them and they are sometimes difficult to enforce. Education is the best weapon; demand for authentic items will promote Indian handmade over imitation products.

Most people buy Indian jewelry for several reasons. They like the look and design and enjoy having a unique piece of jewelry that isn't found in every store in every mall around the country. Another reason is that they know they are buying a piece that has been handmade by an Indian artist. They feel they are contributing to keeping this art alive, as well they are! Indian artists don't just practice their art form as a hobby; they make a living with their art. This is how they feed their families and educate their children.

Fakes and frauds in the marketplace have hurt the Indian arts. If artists can't make a living with their work, they will have to abandon it to take jobs in the cities and all of us will lose. The Indian arts are unique in all the world and are one of the few things that are truly "American." From Australia and Europe to Japan, collectors are fascinated by Indian arts.

Consumers can support the arts by following a few principles:

- Buy from a reputable dealer. Roadside stands and traveling shows are gone when you find there is a problem. A store or gallery has to stand behind what it sells or it will go out of business.

- Look for hallmarks indicating artist and tribe (or country of origin if foreign made).

- Have the seller explain hallmarks to you.

- Ask about materials used.

- Ask that information be put in writing. Some people are reluctant to put misinformation in writing. Having a written receipt also gives you evidence if a problem arises later.

- If it doesn't look right, don't buy it.

- If it seems too cheap or too good a deal, realize that good work and good materials can't be done for little or nothing.

- Don't shop where there are perpetual sales (when store owners tell you everything is 60% off). If they were ethical about their pricing, they couldn't afford to sell at a huge discount. If they aren't ethical about their pricing, will they provide ethical infor mation about the maker or origin?

- Educate yourself about what you want to buy, whether jewelry, art, baskets, rugs, etc.

- Don't be afraid to ask questions. If a clerk isn't helpful or the store owner is reluctant to answer, head for the door. People who are interested in the arts, not just the money, will be happy to talk to you and answer questions. They aren't looking for a one-time sale. They want you to be satisfied and hope for your repeat business.

- If in doubt about a purchase, have it appraised by another dealer.

- Ask what return policy the store uses.

Above all, enjoy what you buy. Wear it, display it, and let it bring happy memories and warm feelings whenever you see it. Indian art is part of the individual who makes it and part of a culture that has been drawn on to inspire it!

Additional Resources

Fane, D., Jacknis, I., & Breen, L (1991). *Objects of myth and memory, American Indian art at the Brooklyn Museum.* New York: University of Washington Press.

Highwater, J. (1983) *Arts of the Indian Americas, Leaves from the sacred tree.* New York: Harper and Row.

Johnson, H. (1992). *Guide to the arts of the Americas. Pre-Columbian and American Indian.* New York: Rizzoli Press.

Lewin, R. (1988). *In the age of mankind.* Washington, DC: Smithsonian Institution Press.

Lister, R. & Lister, F. (1981) *Chaco canyon.* Albuquerque: University of New Mexico.

Powell, J.W. (1881). *First Annual report of the bureau of ethnology.* Washington, DC: Government Printing Office.

Rosnek, C. & Stacy, J. (1976). *Skystone and Silver: The collector's book of southwest Indian jewelry.* Englewood Cliffs, NJ: Prentice-Hall.

Simpson, B. (1974). *Minerals and rocks.* Boston: Galahad Books.

A Jeweler's Story

I was born July 17, 1949, the third of five children, and raised in Isleta Pueblo. My mother was a registered nurse from Isleta Pueblo and my father was a judge for the Navajo Nation from Window Rock, Arizona. I attended Isleta Elementary, grades 1 and 2, then Bosque Farms Elementary. From there I attended Los Lunas high school until I graduated in 1968. I attended New Mexico State University in Las Cruces, New Mexico, for one year, until my draft number came up and I joined the Marine Corps in 1969. Uncle Sam sent me to California, then to Viet Nam for my senior trip. When I returned back home in 1971, I worked for awhile delivering furniture in Albuquerque.

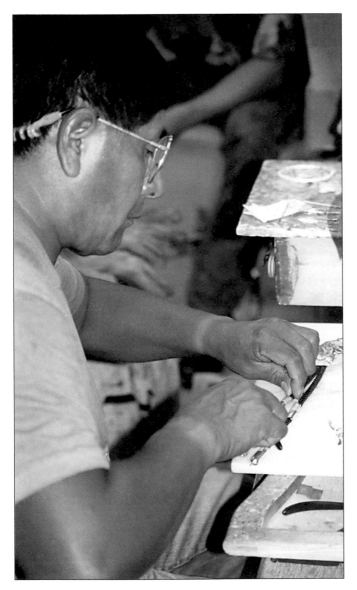

Michael Kirk

Later, I started work at the Southwest Indian Polytechnic Institute. At that time my older brother, Andy, was attending the University of New Mexico and taking jewelry classes. He began to teach me how to make jewelry and one day he said to me, "Let's start a jewelry business." Being young and foolish, I naturally said, "Okay."

We started making jewelry on our mom's kitchen table. In the evening when she got home from work, she would chase us off her table and complain that we were ruining it. We opened our first shop which lasted for seven years. I then worked in heavy equipment for a couple of years until I was involved in an auto accident which fractured my neck. I was told by the doctors that I couldn't work heavy equipment any longer. Thanks to my wife, my brother, and my mother, who all stood by me, I started making jewelry again.

In the beginning, the early 70s, our work was heavy silver and turquoise set in bezel. We later evolved into making small curved leaves and punched-out circles of silver dapped and stamped to look like flowers. Around this time, I made my first feathers. I remember attempting to enter a jewelry show in Albuquerque. I was "tossed out" by a little individual who said they were too perfect. Twenty some-odd years later, I'm still making the same leaves and feathers.

Nowadays, my designs are a mixture of traditional and contemporary. I believe that in the 70s, when everyone and their cousin was in the business, helped fuel the Southwest jewelry craze. The consequential "crash" of this industry helped to weed out both artists and dealers who were not truly involved in it. More recently, we have been assaulted by imports of "look alike" or "Southwestern style" jewelry, rugs, katsina dolls, pottery, and beads from Mexico and the Pacific Rim countries. This has hurt the industry as a whole because both artists and dealers are selling these look-alikes and passing them off as authentic Indian made. This hurts the individual artists because the dealers don't know if the work is genuine or not. This hurts the dealers because the public as a whole doesn't know who to trust.

Very few persons can say they truly enjoy what they do for a living. I am one of these fortunate few. Not only do I get to express myself artistically, but it also brings into play my culture through my designs. While a lot of what we make has to do with our culture, I believe that as an art form it must also be allowed to continue to change and expand. New ideas should be formed and created. Without change comes decay. Young artists should be encouraged and helped along. It is very important to the Native American people, both as an income and as an outpouring of our culture and ideas, that we share our art form with the rest of the world. While it has provided for me and my family, I am especially proud my children have decided to continue in my footsteps. I have won a few ribbons and awards and I am most proud to have won the Artist of the Year award from the Indian Arts and Crafts Association. This is because artists are judged by their peers and there is no greater award that an aspiring artist can enjoy than acceptance by his or her peers. The good Lord willing and the creek doesn't rise, this art form will continue.

Michael Kirk

Pueblo Pottery

Charles King

Miniature pottery.

Pottery is part of the culture and historical background of the indigenous people of the Southwest. There are three important factors that go into each piece of pottery—the clay, the formation of the vessel, and the firing. Each of these aspects of pottery help to distinguish the authentic from the commercial and non-hand crafted pottery.

Making Traditional Pottery

The clay is critical to both the formation of a piece of pottery, as well as to the individual potters. Many of the artists believe that the "Clay Lady" is the spiritual force behind their pottery. They may make a corn meal offering to her when they begin to search and collect their clay. Typically, the clay is dug from areas near the artist's pueblo. It is then taken home and put through a filtering process, which removes larger particles and leaves the finer clay. This process may take several weeks to accomplish. Temper, in the form of volcanic ash or ground pottery shards, is then added to the clay and the process of building the pottery can begin.

Each piece of pottery is built in the traditional coil method. The clay is rolled out into coils and stacked one on another. The coils are then smoothed out and the bowl is sanded and left to dry. After several days of drying, the polishing begins with a wet coat of clay, called a slip, which is applied to the bowl. This slip is polished with a stone to create a high luster. The polishing process is very time consuming, but it is worth the effort. The more time spent polishing, the shinier the bowl will become after it is fired.

Bowl built with the traditional coil method.

When the polishing is complete, the designs can be painted or cut into the clay. Paints are typically made from plant and mineral compounds. Black designs are usually made with Rocky Mountain beeplant or tansy mustard, regional plants which are boiled down to a solid, then ground up and mixed with water to make a paint. Other colors are typically the result of different-colored clay.

Polishing stones.

There are two ways the designs are cut out of the clay. A piece can be carved, resulting in deep grooves which create a design. The incising or "sgraffito" process is also utilized: the potter scratches away at the surface of the bowl with a knife. Typically, incised designs are very intricate and ornate. The incising of a bowl can be done either before or after firing, depending on the depth the artist wishes to achieve. Then, when the bowl is completely designed, it is ready to be fired.

Firing is the final stage in making pueblo pottery. The firing process is always risky because the bowl may crack, break, or even explode during the firing. The defects may be the result of poorly mixed clay or air bubbles in the bowl. Many potters worry about losing pottery in the firing process and frequently may only fire one bowl at a time!

Each pueblo has a different method of firing, but the general process is the same. An outdoor bonfire is constructed using wood, tin, and old pottery shards. These items are used to surround the bowl and keep it out of the flames of the fire. The bowl is usually positioned in the center of the bonfire and wood or dung is stacked around it and set on fire. This firing process can take several hours of work, as the potter has to watch the fire and make certain that it does not die down too quickly. They must also watch the wind, and make certain that it does not fan

Typically, black designs are made with Rocky Mountain beeplant or tansy mustard, regional plants which are boiled down to a solid, and then ground up and mixed with water to make a paint.

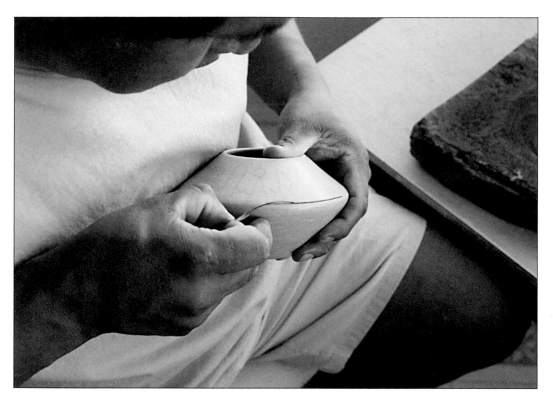

Creating the design on a stone polished bowl.

the flames during the firing. This is one reason why many potters prefer to fire very early in the morning before there is much wind. As the fire begins to die down, the potter then has to let the ashes cool down before seeing what has happened to the bowl. This entire process of firing is similar at each pueblo, except at Santa Clara and San Ildefonso, where they create their famous black ware. In this case, at the end of the firing process, the fire is smothered with manure. This smothering removes the oxygen from around the pottery and results in the black coloration so admired by collectors.

When a bowl is taken out of the fire, it is carefully examined by the potter for cracks, chips and discoloration. There is little they can do at this time to remedy any problems. However, more often than not, when the ashes are cleared away from the fire and the bowl is removed, it is a spectacular work of art, several weeks in the making.

Non-Handcrafted or Commercial Pottery

Pueblo pottery is made using the three basic procedures: gathering the clay, forming the bowl, and firing the bowl. In any one of these steps,

The outdoor bonfire is constructed using wood, tin, and old pottery shards. These items are used to surround the bowl and keep it out of the flames of the fire.

The bowl is usually positioned in the center of the bonfire, and the wood or dung is stacked around it and set on fire.

When the ashes are cleared away from the fire and the bowl is removed, it is a spectacular work of art, several weeks in the making. This bowl was created by Mark Tahbo.

Unfired clay bowl with Beeplant black.

Finished bowl.

or any combination of them, there are ways for the potter to avoid the difficulty of handmaking a piece of pottery.

The process of gathering and filtering the clay is very time consuming and strenuous for the potters, and as a result, some potters are now utilizing commercial clay. This allows the potter to make more unusual shapes and make the pieces more quickly since no is time spent in letting the clay sit while it is being sifted. It also leaves out any impurities which might cause the bowl to crack or fire improperly. However, the use of commercial clay leaves out the critical step of gathering the clay. To most potters, while other stages may be altered, the spiritual aspect of gathering the clay is of great personal importance. As a result, there are very few pueblo potters who do utilize commercial clay. It is typically the non-pueblo potters who are using this type of clay. The use of commercial clay is often difficult to spot, but can sometimes be detected in the size and the weight of a piece. If it is used, it is typically for white pottery, such as Acoma or Laguna or the tan pottery from Hopi.

The use of commercial clay is often paired with the use of a wheel to throw the pottery, instead of the traditional coil method. There has been no historic use of a wheel in the making of Native American Indian pueblo pottery. The use of a wheel instead of coiling often results in a thinner, larger bowl. There are typically more unusual shapes as well. The traditional clay of the pueblos is rarely of the right consistency for wheel throwing and commercial clay has to be used.

Bowl by Hopi-Tewa potter Rondina Huma.

Potters are also turning to the use of commercial ceramics, commonly called "greenware" bought in craft stores. These greenware pieces are formed by pouring the clay into a plaster mold which gives the piece a perfect shape. This relieves the artist not only from having to process the clay, but from having to shape a bowl. As a result, the collector may notice that there are multiple pieces with exactly the same shape. If the piece has not been properly poured and sanded, then there may also be a ridge on the bowl from the casting. When looking inside a cast bowl, there is typically a very white interior, a contrast to the native clay bowl which has more pink coloration.

The cast pottery is typically fired in a kiln. However, bowls that are hand coiled may also be kiln fired. The difference between kiln firing and traditional firing is the risk of breakage; many potters who utilize kiln firing note that it reduces their chance of breakage by 90%! The opportunity to keep pieces from breaking is often enough to motivate potters to use a commercial kiln. However, the results are often not as rich as traditional firing. In Hopi-Tewa pottery, the use of a kiln removes "fire clouds" from the pottery. In such pottery, it is the fire cloud which gives the piece a rich appearance and a depth of color. In pottery from Santa Clara and San Ildefonso, a kiln can only be used on red ware pottery. It is very difficult to tell the difference between kiln fired and traditionally fired red ware pottery. The black pottery must still be traditionally fired in an outdoor bonfire. Kiln firing is most typical on Acoma and Laguna pottery where the potter is attempting to achieve an even white coloration. It is often thought that a kiln fired bowl can be detected by "dinging" the side of pieces and the differences in pitch will determine how the bowl was fired. This practice is highly discouraged, most business owners and artists dislike the practice as it can potentially damage the bowl. The most reliable option is asking the artist or working with a reliable business, which differentiates between kiln and traditionally fired pottery.

Two deep carved vases by Santa Clara Pueblo potter LuAnn Tafoya. The vase on the left is a wedding vase.

This bowl by Mark Tahbo, is fired in the traditional manner, with an out-door fire, displays the characteristic "fire clouds."

It is best to remember that, while a potter may seem prolific, the better they are, the fewer pieces they are able to make in a year. Many of the better known potters may make only between 30 and 40 pieces each year!

Collecting pottery is a deeply rewarding experience. There is a wonderful blend of the aesthetic appearance of a well-made bowl combined with the tactile sense of a three dimensional object. With some time spent learning about the process of making pottery, collectors should feel confident to ask the right questions and enjoy collecting this dynamic area of Native American art.

Deeply carved black vase and egg by Nathan Youngblood of Santa Clara.

Traditionally fired bowl by Hopi-Tewa potter Mark Tahbo, with butterflies pattern originated by his great-grandmother Grace Chapella.

Large bowl by Susan Folwell, of Santa Clara Pueblo, with incised and painted polychrome Northwest Coast designs.

Contemporary vase by San Ildefonso potter Russell Sanchez which incorporates multiple slips, heishi beads and copper leafing.

Large olla with carved and incised designs, by Susan Folwell, Santa Clara.

Additional Resources

Rick Dillingham. *Acoma and Laguna Pottery*. A book focused on the pottery of these two pueblos by the late author of Seven Families in Pueblo Pottery and Fourteen Families in Pueblo Pottery.

Rick Dillingham. *Fourteen Families in Pueblo Pottery*. University of New Mexico Press, Albuquerque, NM. Chronicles the potters and their work and shows how the craft is passed down through the generations. Heavily illustrated with color and black -and-white photos.

Hopi and Hopi-Tewa Pottery. Museum of Northern Arizona, Flagstaff, AZ. A compilation of articles for the Museum of Northern Arizona's *Plateau* magazine. This small book includes the history of Hopi pottery, the pottery techniques and materials, and a discussion of some of the makers.

Navajo Pottery. Museum of Northern Arizona, Flagstaff, AZ. A compilation of articles for the Museum of Northern Arizona's *Plateau* magazine. This small book includes the history of Navajo pottery, a demonstration of technique, and discussions of some of the important Navajo potters.

Mark Bahti. *Pueblo Stories and Storytellers.* Treasure Chest Publications, Tucson, AZ. This book combines the making of the storyteller with the storytelling tradition. Bahti provides various pueblo stories.

Incised seedpot by Santa Clara potter Debra Trujillo-Duwyenie.

Barbara A. Babcock, Guy and Doris Monthan. *The Pueblo Storyteller.* University of Arizona Press, Tucson, AZ, and London, England. A listing of the pottery families with a storyteller tradition and where they learned.

Betty LeFree. (1968). *Santa Clara Pottery Today.* University of New Mexico Press, Albuquerque, NM. A very good demonstration of the pottery-making process.

Stephen Trimble. (1993) *Talking with the Clay—The Art of Pueblo Pottery.* School of American Research Press, Santa Fe, NM.

Gregory Schaff. (1998). *Hopi-Tewa Pottery, 500 Artists Biographies.* Center for Indigenous Arts & Culture Press, Santa Fe NM.

Susan Peterson. (1997). *Pottery by American Indian Women.* Abbeville Press and The National Museum of Women in the Arts.

A Hopi-Tewa Potter

Mark Tahbo comes from one of the three leading families of Hopi-Tewa potters. He is the great-grandson of noted potter Grace Chapella. She was known for her large-sized pieces and the revival of the butterfly or moth design on the pottery. Grace was already over 100 years old when Mark became interested in ceramics. While she was not able to instruct him on the intricacies of making pottery, her memory and legacy continue to be a source of inspiration to him.

Mark's pottery reflects the history and the tradition of the Hopi-Tewa people. This can be seen in the pottery's form as well as in the designs. The tradition is also an integral part of how Mark makes his pottery, building his pieces in the coil method, painting them with natural paints, and firing them outdoors. Mark learned much of his pottery-making skills on his own. Trial and error has led to a process of discovery which makes each piece more refined than the last.

Innovation is the key to Mark's pottery. He has developed his own techniques for firing that allow him to achieve a rich "fire cloud" or blush that encompasses his bowls. His designs are bold but flowing with each piece able to stand on its own as an independent work of art. His form ranges from classical to his own innovative shapes. Mark spends a great deal of time designing his pottery, so that the patterns will complement the form. The final results are impressive and each piece of pottery is an aesthetic delight for the viewer.

In addition to his own work, Mark has influenced many younger members of his family to take up pottery making. He willingly shares his knowledge of bowl construction, painting and firing

Mark Tahbo

to help them achieve the best final results. Mark says, "It is important to encourage and bring along the next generation. They will keep alive the traditions and history in their work. However, it is important to have them make their pottery in the traditional method. Kiln firing, acrylic paints, cast pottery—these are the temptations for younger potters. If they focus on quality and their traditions, they will be able to achieve much."

Throughout his career Mark has won numerous awards for his work at events such as Santa Fe Indian Market, Gallup Inter-Tribal Ceremonials and the Heard Museum Indian Market. He has achieved recognition in books such as *Talking with the Clay, Fourteen Families in Pueblo Pottery,* and *The Art of the Hopi, Hopi-Tewa Pottery.* His work has been featured on the front cover of *Southwest Art* magazine.

A Mark Tahbo bowl emerges from the firing process.

Navajo Rugs

Georgiana Kennedy Simpson

Priscilla Sagg weaving.

Watching a Navajo weaver work at her loom is a lesson in patience and perseverance. A weaver sits before her tapestry for hours transforming the geometric equation in her mind into a beautiful rug design. Practitioners of this form of weaving talk about the meditation which takes place when they lose themselves in the weaving. Unlike the loud bang of a horizontal loom as each row of wool yarn is pushed into place, a weaver sitting before the traditional vertical loom of the Navajo breaks the silence with the gentle swish of the comb tamping down the wool threads. Fingers hold the comb and move the battens patiently and endlessly in the creation of the woven rug. Unlike other types of looms that make it easier for the weaver to manipulate the pressure and hasten the movement of the yarn, the very nature of the Navajo loom makes the production of a Navajo rug a 100% handmade process. The "pinkie callous" on a weaver's hand is a badge of Navajo weaving artistry.

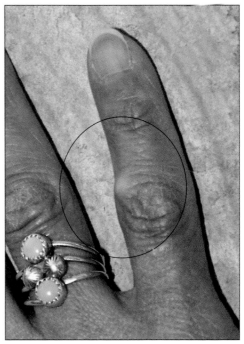

The "pinkie callous" on a weaver's hand.

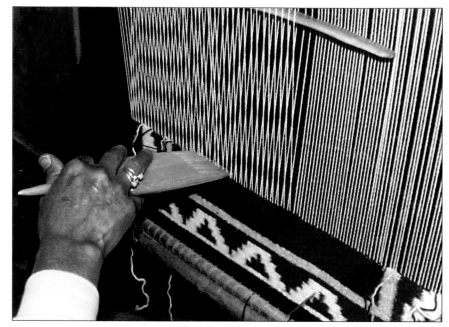

Comb tamping the wool threads.

Origin

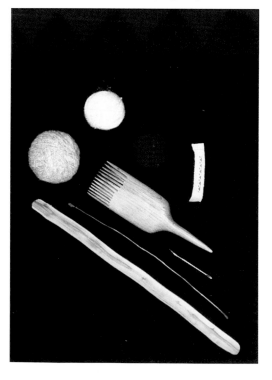

The Navajo people arrived in the Southwest before the Spanish (who first arrived in the 1500s). Spanish and Mexican style weaving took place on the horizontal loom, a ponderous contraption. The Navajo weavers learned from the pueblo people of the Southwest. The pueblo loom was a simple device and easily moved—an important attribute for the early Navajo lifestyle. Although pueblo men were traditionally the weavers, in Navajo culture, it was the women who evolved into the predominant weavers.

Along with pottery and baskets, blankets were utilitarian items. Early weaving focused on the making of sashes, dresses and blankets. The introduction of the railroad in the 1880s and the establishment of trading posts on the newly created Navajo reservation set the stage for an artistic boom which continues

Weaving tools: batten, needles, warp yarn, comb, weaving yarn, design sample.

"Male and Female Corn," with weaver, Eleanor Yazzie.

today. Hand-woven blankets were replaced with - ever early travelers to the Southwest saw the beautiful weavings and wanted to buy them. The conversion from blanket to rug began in the late 1800s as collectors acquired the weavings as floor coverings, wall decorations, and bed spreads.

Early traders played a great role in the marketing of Navajo weavings by providing an outlet for wool, sheep, and weavings. Arrangements with wholesale houses such as C.N. Cotton's location in Gallup, NM, gave the outlying traders a place to trade in the wool products for merchandise. Catalogs distributed by Lorenzo Hubbell in Ganado, AZ, C.N. Cotton in Gallup, and J.B. Moore in Crystal, NM, brought widespread attention to this art of the southwest.

Anglo influence on early designs, colors, and patterns started immediately. Lorenzo Hubbell favored deep reds and combed natural gray. With the help of various painters, he distributed designs to the weavers. J.B. Moore, a trader at the Crystal Trading Post, introduced different patterns to the weavers of that area, some appearing to have an Oriental influence. Market demand largely determined which designs, patterns, and colors would become established or fade into oblivion. Commercial yarns were available as early as the late 1800s with the introduction of Germantown yarns. The use of these yarns caused an explosion of color and design which can be seen in some of today's Teec Nos Pos, Red Mesa, and Germantown revival weavings. Many weavers stayed with the natural yarns and a color palette which consisted mostly of black, brown, red, gray, and white. In the 1940s, Sally Lippincott of the Wide Ruins Trading Post encouraged the use of natural plant dyes which produced weavings of soft, beautiful colors. These natural colors and their synthetic equivalents can be seen in today's Chinle, Wide Ruins, Burntwater, and Crystal weavings.

A few decades ago, many lamented the potential demise of Navajo weaving. The task of making a rug was arduous and time consuming and the weaver was often paid pennies per hour for her efforts. Fortunately, the wide distribution of commercial yarns has helped correct this economic difficulty for the weaver. With fine wools available to the weaver, she can put her time into the warping of the loom and weaving of the rug. With the ability to focus on the technical aspects of weaving, artists are producing some of the finest quality work seen in the history of Navajo weaving. Approximately five percent of the rugs woven today are still done with natural, hand spun wools, and weavers of these rugs should be recognized for their extra efforts.

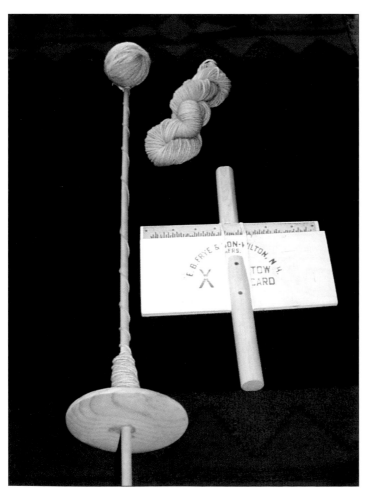

Carding and spinning tools.

Weaving

Weaving a rug is an arduous task, especially for weavers who process their own wool and use natural dyes. The weaving tradition is most often passed down in families. Many families on the reservation raise sheep and goats. If they process their own wool, the sheep is shorn and the wool is washed. The wool is then carded between two carding combs. These straightened strands are then taken and hand spun on a simple hip spindle. If any commercial or natural dyes are to be used, the yarn is typically dyed at this time.

Early looms typically consisted of logs and branches constructed into a rectangular, upright structure. This type of loom is still quaintly depicted in miniature versions of weaver dolls. However, today a loom is more exactly engineered with smooth pipes and finished lumber in order for the weaver to execute a more symmetrical rug. The weaver must decide in advance the exact length and width of the rug, since the ends or selvage must be attached before the weaving begins. Weavings produced on this type of loom are unique because they have four closed edges. Rugs woven on any other type of loom can only have two.

Any good weaver will tell you the warping of the loom is most important. Setting up a consistent warp sets the foundation for a balanced and smooth weaving. A weaver wraps the warp in a figure eight pattern stretched between two temporary beams. The spun yarn used for the actual weaving is referred to as the weft. The vast majority of Navajo rugs are 100 percent wool or wool with some mohair carded in. The only exceptions are some inexpensive runners woven in the Gallup, NM, area which use wool for the weft and cotton threads for the warp. Occasionally, a weaver will use an acrylic yarn, but this happens rarely, since these rugs are found to be undesirable by today's collector.

After warping is complete, the loom is raised upright. One or more heddles and a shed stick are put into place. These simple tools are used to separate the warp threads from front to back creating a "shed" which allows the weft thread to pass through the warp. The warp is then stretched to the tension needed and the weaving may begin.

Tapestry weave, employed in weaving most Navajo rugs, means over one warp, under one warp. The exception to this technique are twills. A weaver places a strand of yarn between warp threads held open by a batten, a smooth stick to hold the shed open. The batten allows the weaver to separate a specific number of warp threads in order to run a particular color of yarn through the warp. Depending on the weaver's technique, the batten is either left

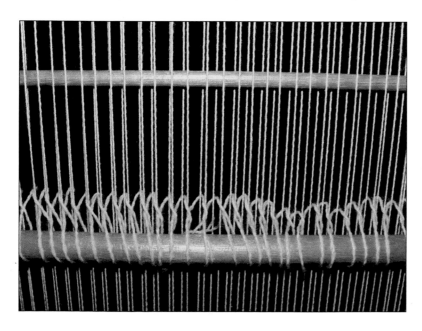

Heddle & shed stick.

Priscilla Sagg opening the shed.

horizontal or is flattened and a comb is used to tamp down the threads. One of the great joys of watching an accomplished weaver is her ability to translate a complex geometric pattern from her head to her "blank sheet of paper," the warped loom.

As a weaver nears completion of the weaving, the most difficult part of the weaving begins. The area left to weave becomes much smaller and tighter. The last part of the weaving may take a long time to complete as it requires the weft to be taken through the warp one stitch at a time all the way up to the selvage edge. Various needles are often employed at this point as the space becomes too tight for the weaver's fingers. The mark of an accomplished weaver is apparent in her ability to control the tension of her weaving at this point to where the rug does not roll or become narrower because this part of the weaving was not properly executed.

Imitations

As Navajo rugs became wildly popular and their value increased, the door opened for imitations, predominantly weavings produced in Mexico. The weavings from Mexico can be collector items due to their own fine quality. The problem occurs when an unscrupulous vendor or artist tries to sell a Mexican weaving as the typically more valuable Navajo rug.

Predominant designs such as Yeis, Storms, and Chief patterns have been introduced to weavers in Mexico. These artisans can reproduce the patterns more quickly on horizontal looms and at much cheaper labor rates. Look for these particular characteristics in order to identify Mexican weaving.

• Mexican weavings typically have multiple warp threads running along each vertical edge of the weaving. A Navajo rug will only have a

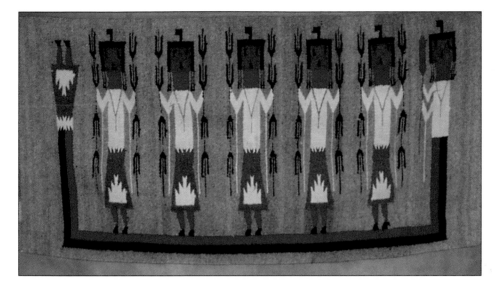

Is it a Navajo or Mexican rug? (Answer: Mexican)

single warp thread running on the vertical selvage of the rug. Gently separate the weft threads on the vertical edge of the weaving to see if there is a single warp thread. Ask store owners or artists about doing this first in order not to offend them.

• Mexican weavings often possess a fringe on each end of the rug where the rug is cut from the loom. The horizontal loom can run a continuous warp whereas each Navajo rug is individually warped.

Remember the Navajo rug has four closed selvage edges. Some weavers have gotten around this by sewing the fringe back into the weaving. So again, gently separate the weft threads on each end of the rug and check for a fringe sewn back inside the weaving. The fringe would only go back into the weaving about an inch.

The selvage on a Mexican blanket. Mexican weavings typically have multiple warp threads running along each vertical edge of the weaving.

Gently separate the weft threads on the vertical edge of the weaving to see if there is a single warp thread.

Knotted tassels on a Mexican blanket. Mexican weavings often possess a fringe on each end of the rug where the rug is cut from the loom.

Knot at the end of Mexican weaving. The fringe of this weaving has been pushed back inside the rug.

Tips for Collecting

Excellent books exist on the various regional styles developed in Navajo weaving. Especially now, weavers from different regions are making every type of rug. Many new patterns and variations are emerging which makes this current period one of the most dynamic in the history of Navajo weaving.

Below are some guidelines to help you navigate the sometimes intimidating world of Navajo rug collecting.

1. Educate yourself on how an authentic Navajo rug looks and feels. Wool has a particular character and you can look for particular things which distinguish wool from other fibers. It is not as easy as it sounds. Handling as many rugs as possible will give you a sense for authentic Navajo weaving.

2. Buy from reputable dealers and artists. Going to a knowledgeable source can be the single most important action of your weaving education. This point may sound silly, but rug buying horror stories often involve misrepresentation at the retail level, whether it be at a roadside stand where you thought you were buying from an actual weaver or stores where the profit incentive overpowers the ethical representation of the weavings.

3. Understand the technique of weaving in order to look for a better quality of rug. Ask yourself the following questions: Is the weaving straight? Are the corners square? Are the patterns consistent and centered within the rug? Does the rug lie flat? Are there gaps in the weft which allow the warp to show through? Is the overall balance of the design good?

These next points discuss particular aesthetics of the weaving. Some collectors place less value on these in weaving, but must be considered on a personal basis.

1. Does the rug possess noticeable lazy lines? Lazy lines are created when a weaver works on a particular section of a rug, rather than weaving the full width one row at a time. Very good weavers may weave in this manner, but are skilled at concealing where these lines occur. Lazy lines are often apparent in older weavings and for some, add to the character of that weaving. Collectors of contemporary weavings usually do not wish for these lines to be noticeable.

2. Are the colors consistent? Again, with older weavings, color variations often add to the interest of the rug, if not the value. It is not uncommon for an older weaving to have variations of gray throughout the rug as the weaver carded different batches of black and white wool to weave into the rug or dyed separate batches of red. This color variation does not happen as frequently now because weavers purchase the commercially-dyed yarns. Even so, pay attention to the color throughout the rug in case a weaver ran out of a particular color and substituted a similar color in its place.

Additional Resources

Amsden, C.A. (1934) *Navaho weaving—its technic and its history*. Glorieta, NM: Rio Grande Press.

Bennett, N. (1979). *Working with the wool*. Flagstaff, AZ: Northland Press.

Berlant, A. & Kahlenbert, M.H. (1977). *Walk in beauty—The Navajo and their blankets*. Boston: New York Graphic Society.

Bonar, E.H. (Ed.). (1996). *Woven by the grandmothers*. New York: National Museum of the American Indian.

Dockstader, F.J. (1987) *The song of the loom*. New York: Hudson Hills Press.

Hedlund, A.L. (1992) *Reflections of the weaver's world*. Denver: Denver Art Museum.

McManis, K. & Jeffries, R. (1997). *A guide to Navajo weavings*. Tucson, AZ: Treasure Chest Books.

Williams, L.L. (1989). *C.N. Cotton and his Navajo blankets*. Albuquerque, NM: Avanyu Publishing, Inc.

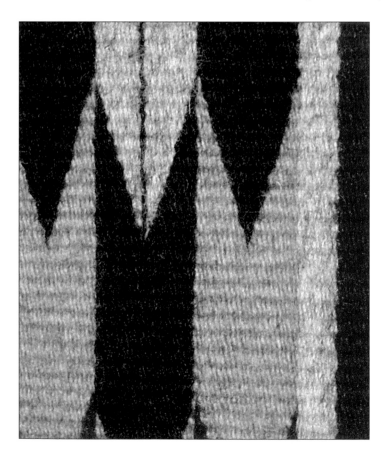

Detail of a weaving by Priscilla Sagg.

A Navajo Weaver

Eleanor Yazzie was born in 1963 at Keams Canyon, AZ, to Joe and Ella Benally. She has two sisters and five brothers. When visiting her grandmother on her mother's side at Smoke Signal, she would watch her weave. Her grandmother, Bah Begay, especially loved weaving storm pattern rugs.

Eleanor helped her grandmother who, at that time, made handspun rugs. Eleanor learned every step from shearing the sheep to washing and dyeing the wool to spinning the yarn. Because her grandmother especially loved the storm pattern weavings, this was the first type she wove. Her mastery of complex geometrics and diagonal lines comes from this early experience in weaving the storm pattern.

One of the added dimensions to this particular style of artwork is the manner in which weaving is learned. Rather than being taught in a formal setting, Navajo weaving is usually part of the overall fabric of their lives. Children are raised watching

Eleanor Yazzie with her rug, "Stars over the Red Rock."

grandmothers, mothers, and aunts working at their looms. After years of helping and watching her grandmother and mother weave, Eleanor attempted her first rug at the age of fifteen. A pattern seems to run in her family for weaving starting in the adolescent years. Her brother, Gabriel, wove his first rug at the age of fifteen. He is one of a handful of Navajo men who have taken up the art of weaving. Two of her sisters, Shirley James and Geraldine Benally, are weavers as well. Her daughter, Carnelda, started weaving when she was twelve years old and now, at the age of sixteen, is capable of weaving some of the more complex geometric designs. Eleanor says of her daughter's weaving development, "Carnelda would help me either weave part of my rug or warp the loom. I am still helping her learn how to properly string the warp. She likes to weave rugs in natural colors and red with stairstep designs."

Eleanor weaves every day, except for the days she is travelling to sell her rugs. She has five children ranging in ages from nine to sixteen years old, so she takes advantage of the quiet time when her children are in school. When asked why she weaves, Eleanor responds, "I like weaving. I don't want to just sit around. My kids are all in school and it keeps me busy." Her favorite size to weave is a 4' by 6' rug, although she can make one up to 5½' wide and as long as needed. The size of her current loom doesn't allow for any wider weavings. When weaving, she likes to listen to gospel music. She looks at her weaving as a way of praising the Lord.

She is currently working on a number of new designs, like corn figures woven into the rug. Her father, Joe Benally, likes the designs she is weaving today as they remind him of old patterns. She used to work in the natural and red colors and would never have thought of making a rug with a black background until a couple of years ago. Her creativity has been rewarded. At the 1998 Gallup Ceremonial, she swept the awards for the Special Design or Function category.

The hands of Eleanor Yazzie, rug weaver.

Baskets

Georgiana Kennedy Simpson

Before silver jewelry, before pottery and before rug weaving, there was basketry. When collectors think of American Indian art, baskets often get relegated to the background. However, baskets are one of the earliest craft forms of the ancestors of today's Native American people. Archaeologists often speak of the excitement in finding a basket among prehistoric ruins. It is almost beyond reason how an item made entirely of organic material can survive the ravages of time.

The great durability of the ancient baskets can be witnessed in many museum collections today: storage baskets found in pristine condition or woven sandals from millennium-old ruins. The striking characteristic of baskets lies in the construction of sturdy vessels out of seemingly flexible and temporary foundations. Today, basket making is experiencing a renaissance, albeit a struggling one, in various parts of the country. Although this book is subtitled *Traditional Work of the Southwest* in this section baskets from all over the United States are discussed. The authenticity issues which affect so much of the Indian art of the Southwest are a problem for basketmakers nationwide, so broader scope was taken in this area.

Origin

The ancient people of North America developed various tools to aid them in their food gathering and storage. By utilizing the native vegetation, practical vessels were constructed for helping with the harvest and storage of seeds and plant materials. Willows were lashed together and woven to create other useful items such as cradleboards for babies and sandals for their feet. The knowledge and use of local plants has always been an integral part of the survival of people in North America. The Industrial Age and advent of mass production made this type of knowledge less crucial; however, many Native Americans have held tightly to their teachings of nature.

In the lexicon of Southwestern archaeologists, before the "Pueblo" phases, you have the "Basketmakers." This delineation is important in the progression from baskets as the major storage vessels to the introduction and increased use of pottery. Pottery making techniques were introduced from groups in what is now Mexico. In the more pristine ruins of the Southwest, it is not unusual to find bits of twine. Most weaving now viewed in private and public collections makes you appreciate the ingenuity of the craftsmen. In the Southwest, strips of cottonwood served as swaddling for babies; in the Northeast, split ash provided the splints for containers; in the Southeast, river cane provided the material for plaited baskets and mats; in the Northwest, fibers were woven into fine bags.

Because of the advent of so many preferable storage containers, combined with the hard work of making baskets, basketmaking struggles or has died out among many of the native tribes. Fortunately, interested tribes and supportive traders and collectors have helped revive basketmaking in many parts of the country. Some weavers have formed cooperatives, such as the Maine Basketmakers Association or the Qualla Art Cooperative (Cherokee, NC) to sustain the artists. California basketmakers are in the midst of a grueling revival which has been greatly aided by their cooperation in the California Basketmakers Association. A strong market in the Southwest, originally encouraged by the Fred Harvey Company in the early 1900s, has helped sustain basketmaking in that area of the country. Today, the success of Navajo, Tohono O'Odham, and Apache basketmakers has been largely encouraged by area traders.

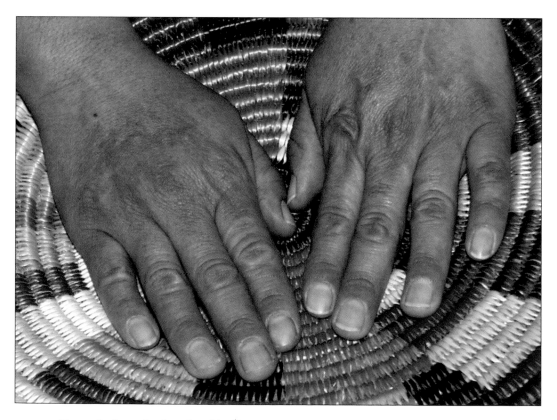

If you look at the hands of basketmakers, you can see they are very strong.

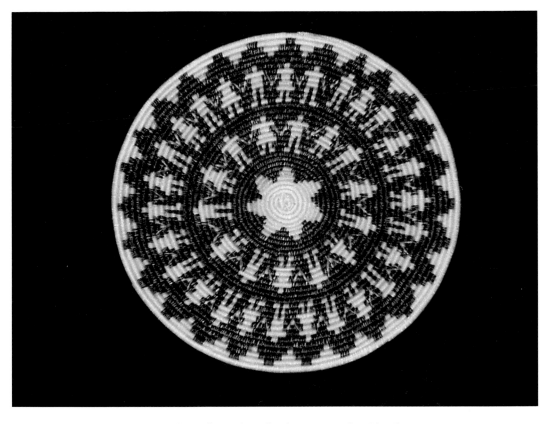

Tohono O'Odham horsehair basket woven by Charlene Juan.

Making a Basket

So, what's the big deal about baskets anyway? Why the fuss? If you have ever attempted to make a Native American style basket, you already know the answer to the question. Great hand strength is needed for working the materials and bending them to the form you need. If you look at the hands of basketmakers, you can see they are very strong. Knowledge of plant sources is a given, not just for finding the materials, as many good basketmakers also cultivate the wild plants for sustained use.

Material preparation is another important element. This usually requires stripping the gathered stalks and splitting them into sewing material. It may sound easy, but acquiring the technique for splitting splints evenly can take years of practice. A great deal of experience is also required to get coils straight or sides straight on a plaited basket. The best basket weavers will constantly push toward a finer coil and a more finished basket, often featuring more complicated designs.

1900s Paiute beaded basket.

Materials

Baskets start with the best materials, which means finding stands of

Miniature Paiute feather and bead basket by Sandra Eagle.

healthy plants. Basketmakers will search far and wide for good materials and will often cultivate the best plants for years of sustained harvesting. This requires an intimate knowledge of the plants. The warp or foundation of the basket may require one kind of plant while the weft or sewing splints may come from another. Dye materials come from yet another source. Some baskets, including those made in northern California, require several types of plants for the weft in order to create designs.

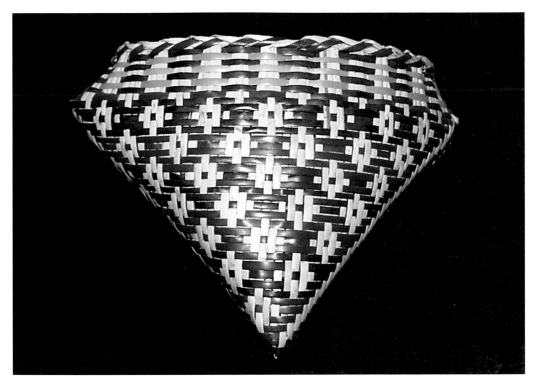

Chitimacha heart basket by Ann Darden.

Animal materials are also utilized in some baskets. The Tohono O'Odham have become famous for finely woven horsehair baskets. Washoe weavers in Nevada and a Chumash weaver in California also use horsehair. Some Eskimo baskets are made from whale baleen. Apache weavers are known for their burden baskets trimmed in leather. The Pomo, Northern Paiute, and Pima weavers loved using beads to adorn their baskets. Pomo, Yokuts, and Paiute weavers also used feathers to adorn their baskets, although this practice is most uncommon today due to the legal restrictions associated with different types of bird feathers.

Techniques

The primary techniques employed in making baskets are **plaiting, coiling,** and **twining.** All baskets found and made by American Indians employ one of these techniques. It is not uncommon for more than one style to be executed by any one tribe.

Plaiting is the simplest of the basket techniques. Flat materials are utilized such as wood splints, split cane, or split yucca. As a child, you may have had an art project requiring the weaving of place mats out of construction paper strips where you laid the strips over and under each other to create a checkerboard effect. This process is the essence of the

Detail of a Hopi utility basket showing plaiting technique.

Hopi utility basket.

Hopi wicker plaque.

Detail of a Hopi wicker plaque.

1920s Hualapai twined basket.

Unusual double start coil by Navajo artist Evelyn Cly.

plaiting technique. Twill plaiting can be seen in Pueblo utility baskets. More complex images can be seen in Chitimacha basketry. There is also a style of plaiting utilized by Hopi weavers from Third Mesa using a round weft element which completely covers the warp material underneath. These baskets are commonly referred to as "wicker" baskets.

Twining is a technique most similar to other weaving techniques, such as Navajo rugs, because it typically involves two flexible weft strands woven around a stiffer warp material. Twined pieces can be very flexible like the weaving done by the Nez Perce, or very stiff like the baskets of the Grand Canyon Hualapai weavers or Apache burden basket makers.

Coiling is most common today in the southwestern United States and California. The foundation is made up of groups of sticks, fiber bundles, or a combination of the two. Split sewing elements are wrapped around the bundle and attached to the previous completed coil.

The coil can consist of a single rod as often found in Pomo baskets and some modern Navajo baskets. It is more common in Navajo baskets today to have three to five rods in the foundation or two rods and a bundle. A bundle of fibers is common in Tohono O'Odham, Hopi, Coushatta, and Eskimo baskets.

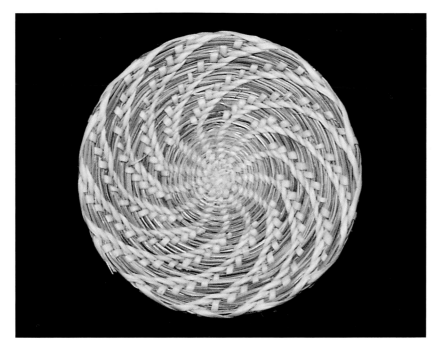

Split stitch yucca and beargrass tray by Tohono O'Odham artist Juanita Xavier.

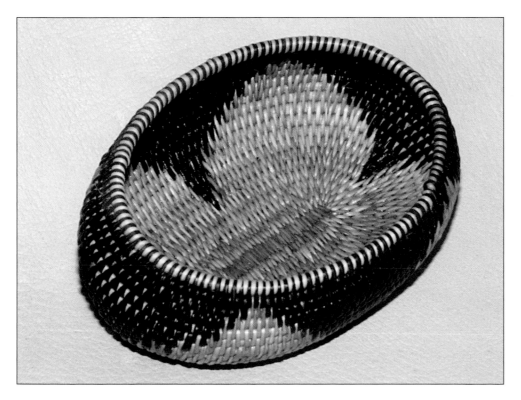

Pomo single rod basket from 1900.

Navajo artist Elsie Holiday single rod weaving technique.

Single rod tray by Navajo artist Elsie Holiday.

Identifying

Baskets have always been in high demand. Native Americans have used baskets heavily for centuries for utilitarian and ceremonial needs. Although other containers such as pottery, and later metal and plastic, replaced the utilitarian function, baskets continue to be important for ceremonial use. The Navajo ceremonial, or more narrowly called the

Navajo wedding basket (left, above and below) vs.
Pakistani look-alike (right, above and below).

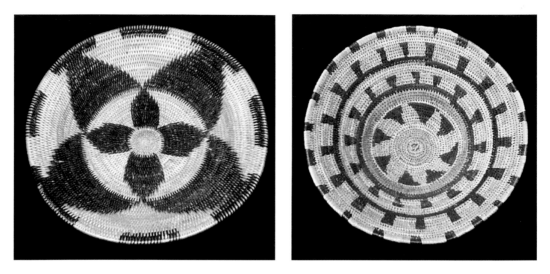

The basket and basket detail on the left is an authentic California Atsegewi basket. The basket and detail on the right is from Africa.

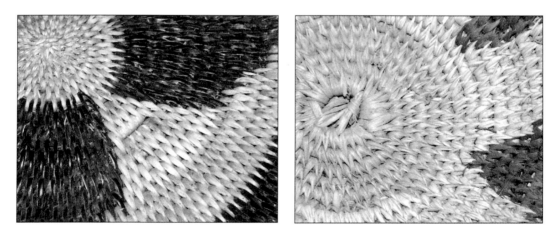

"wedding" basket (so named because of its use in a traditional wedding ceremony) is a perfect example. Demand has always outstripped the supply of baskets available for their ceremonial use. As many artists turned away from the difficult task of basketmaking, the demand and price for baskets continued to climb. Enter foreign-made baskets made to look like the Navajo ceremonial basket. As demand for older Native American baskets skyrocketed, misrepresentation of foreign made baskets became more common.

In identifying a true Native American basket, knowledge of the plant materials, techniques and designs are most important. The only way to truly learn the difference between plant materials used here in

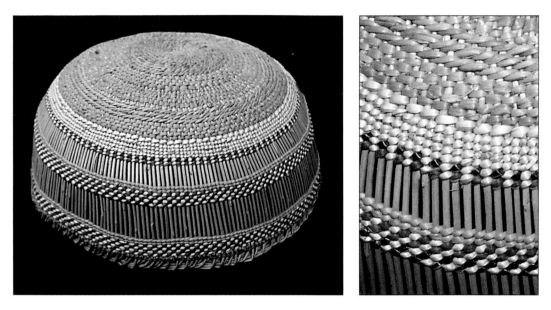

California Hupa Hat (above left and right).

Brazilian look-alike (above left and right).

the United States versus other parts of the world is to handle many baskets, Native American and foreign, in order to better understand the differences. Each type of basketry across this country has a particular signature due to the materials used, the technique applied, and the designs utilized by a particular group.

Fishing creel by Donald and Mary Sanipass.

Collecting and Care

While many basket collectors have rushed to gather older baskets, basketmakers today deserve and desperately need the support of Native American art lovers. Where commercial yarn has been accepted in Navajo rugs and far superior materials and tools are available to the silversmith, and fetish and katsina carver, no shortcuts exist for the

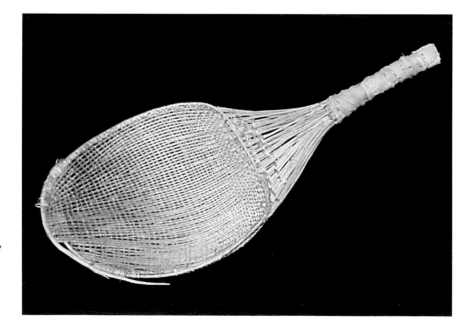

Paiute seedbeater.

Hupa rattle.

Passamaquoddy corn basket by Theresa Neptune Gardner.

Mono cradle board.

basketmaker. Except for the introduction of aniline dyes for some area weavers, the materials must be cultivated and specially prepared. They cannot run down to the local craft shop for supplies. Basketmakers' tools usually consist of little more than a knife, an awl, and the weaver's hands and teeth.

Every basket has its own charm. The simple utility baskets like the Pueblo willow baskets or Paiute seedbeaters have enormous character. Many artists are striving for technical perfection. For example, in the past year, a half dozen Navajo weavers have started making single rod foundation coil baskets which have not been made in almost one hundred years. Basketmakers in California are not only striving for their own technical excellence but are helping many other

Hopi carrying basket.

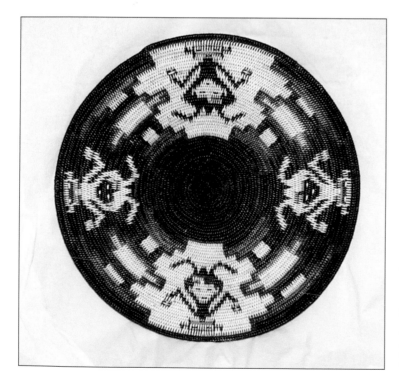

Peter Holiday single rod basket with Navajo depiction of Mother Earth and Father Sky.

weavers learn and progress. As in other art forms, the basket weavers like to look at other weavers' work and determine how the weaver accomplished a particular design or weave.

When looking at a basket for your own collection, first decide what is important to you. Was it woven by a child or one of few weavers working in this particular style? Is this basketmaker responsible for a renaissance of weaving in their area? If technical work is important, look for evenness in the stitches, balance in the design, and what effort a weaver took in finishing a basket. For example, did the weaver trim any loose strands or construct a special rim?

Even though the great durability of baskets was mentioned at the beginning of this section, a few simple steps can prolong the good condition of your basket. Keep baskets out of the direct sunlight. Because of the plant

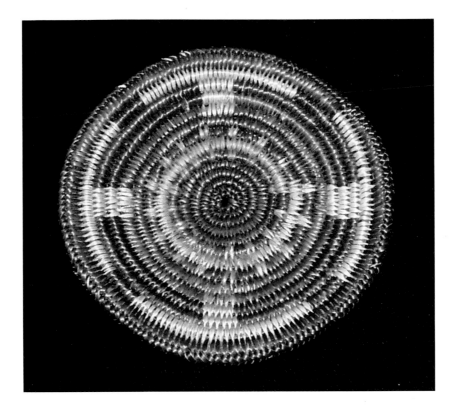

Navajo child's basket made by Angelina Holiday, the ten year old daughter of Navajo basketmakers Elsie and Peter Holiday.

fiber, sun can quickly deteriorate a basket, bleaching out the color and breaking down the material. Keep baskets out of areas where they are likely to collect dirt or grease, like the kitchen. Keep them out of areas which can be excessively damp, such as a bathroom, or excessively dry, such as near a heating vent. Check baskets for any insect damage.

Finally, when handling your baskets, treat them gently. Pick up baskets using both hands. Never pick them up by the rim. Make sure your hands are clean when handling your baskets as they will pick up oils from your skin. Most of all, just enjoy them. Baskets are very aesthetically pleasing to the eye and touch.

Additional Resources

Bates, C.D. & Lee, M.J. (1990). *Tradition and innovation.* Yosemite National Park, CA: Yosemite Association.

Bibby, B. (1996). *The fine art of California Indian basketry.* Sacramento, CA: Crocker Art Museum.

Contemporary artists and craftsmen of Eastern Band of Cherokee Indians. (1987). Cherokee, NC: Qualla Arts and Crafts Mutual, Inc.

Dewald, T. (1979). *The Papago Indians and their basketry.* Tucson: University of Arizona Press.

Edison, C.A. (Ed.) (1996). *Willow stories—Utah Navajo baskets.* Salt Lake City: Utah Arts Council.

Fang, M.W. & Binder, M.R. (1990). *A photographic guide to the ethnographic North American Indian basket collection.* Cambridge, MA: Peabody Museum of Archaeology and Ethnology, Harvard University.

James, G.W. (Ed.) (1909). *Indian basketry.* New York: Dover Publications.

Lobb, A. (1990). *Indian baskets of the Pacific northwest and Alaska.* Portland, OR: Graphic Arts Center Publishing Company.

Mason, O.T. (1970). *Aboriginal Indian basketry.* Glorieta, NM: Rio Grande Press.

Peabody, S. & Turnbaugh, W.A. (1986). *Indian baskets.* West Chester, PA: Schiffer Publishing Ltd.

Remember your relations, The Elsie Allen baskets, family & friends. (1996). Ukiah, CA: Grace Hudson Museum.

Tanner, C.L. (1989). *Indian baskets of the southwest.* Tucson: University of Arizona Press.

Teiwes, H. (1996). *Hopi basket weaving—artistry in natural fibers.* Tucson: University of Arizona Press.

Whiteford, A.H. (1988). *Southwestern Indian baskets.* Santa Fe: School of American Research Press.

Yamane, L. (1997). *Weaving a California tradition.* Minneapolis: Lerner Publications Company

Joann is holding the first two baskets in a Dusk to Dawn series.

A Navajo Basket Weaver

A fourth generation Navajo basket weaver, Joann Johnson has a passionate awareness of her heritage and history. Born and raised in Monument Valley, she has spent her life in the Navajo heartland surrounded by the sacred mountains and monuments that tell the stories of her people's past. Joann feels a responsibility to help preserve that past by preserving her culture. Basket weaving is one way she demonstrates her commitment to her convictions. "It's a gift," she says of her weaving abilities. "I learned it from my mother, who learned from her mother, who learned from her mother, my greatgrandmother, Ida Bigman. I feel close to her when I am weaving a basket."

Joann Johnson received an Associate Degree in Business from the College of Eastern Utah, a two year college, then went on to a university, where she became interested in history, especially Native American history. "I would like to go back and get a degree in history," she says. In the meantime she is preserving history by carrying on a family tradition—that of Navajo basket weaving.

Joann was taught to weave rugs and baskets by her mother when she was about 8 years old. She also learned to crochet and became quite adept at crocheting without having to watch her hands. But of all her talents, basket weaving is one that has brought her the most satisfaction. "Weaving comes naturally for me," she says. Her first place award at the Intertribal Ceremonial (Gallup) backs up her statement.

She only works on her baskets when she is drawn to them—usually in the evening when she is ready to sit down and rest. "When I'm busy, then weaving doesn't relax me," she says. "I do it when I get in the mood, when I want to relax."

Joann also says the money she gets from selling her baskets is not a driving force for her. "It's not the money as much as the accomplishment," she asserts. She enjoys creating beautiful things, taking the ideas that come to her and making them real, bringing them to fruition.

This may be one of the reasons her baskets are so beautiful, because she has such a love for her art. She is modest and yet candid about her baskets. Speaking of the unusual gray color she often uses, she recalls her favorite piece was the first gray basket she finished. "It was really nice," she says honestly. "It came out nice."

Nice is a good word to describe Joann. She has a pleasant personality and infectious laugh. But she is serious when she speaks of her legacy. "The breaking of tradition creates a downfall for people," she says, then emphasizes, "All people. We must stick to our culture."

Joann loves education, developing her talents, and learning new things. She has learned how to make an unusual single rod basket even though it takes more time and uses more materials that the conventional double rod basket, just because she enjoys a unique undertaking. "I like the challenge of a new design," she says.

Joann hopes that the people who buy her baskets will sense the creation of life in them, the energy she gives to them. "I just want them to know it's a part of me," she emphasizes, "I hope they can enjoy it. It's a gift—I hope they will cherish it."

Large rainbow mosaic by Joann Johnson.

Fetish Carvings

Georgiana Kennedy Simpson

This label should be attached to the first fetish anyone buys:

WARNING! COLLECTING FETISHES IS HIGHLY ADDICTIVE.
YOU CANNOT BUY JUST ONE!

Dinosaur carving by Leonard Halate.

Collecting fetishes is highly personal. Speak to one collector and he will tell you about each carving's personality. Another may speak of her attraction to the realistic carvings of the Cheama family. Yet another may enjoy the humor in Leonard Halate's wacky dinosaur carvings. Whatever the attraction, collecting fetishes is extremely popular. For many who want to enjoy the beauty of Native American art but are limited in budget or space, fetish collecting is the perfect solution.

Talismans have been a part of cultures throughout the world. Archaeologists have found figures at sites scattered around the globe. A fetish is an object, natural or man-made, in which a spirit is thought to reside and which can be used to effect either good or evil. The word fetish comes from the Portuguese word "feitico" which comes from the Latin word "facticus" which means artificially produced. For the purposes of

Navajo horse fetish.

this discussion, when we speak of fetishes, we are referring to the animals carved for the consumer market by the people of the southwestern Pueblo cultures. A few carvers produce fetishes at other Pueblo villages, specifically Isleta and Cochiti, but the majority of Native American fetish carvings made for the consumer market today are produced by Zuni carvers.

The Navajo people use fetishes as well. Navajo fetish use concentrates most often on protection animals for their livestock, such as carvings of sheep, horses, and cows. Navajo uranium miners were known to carry badger and mole fetishes for protection. Often Navajos will acquire a pueblo fetish for their use rather than making their own. The vast majority of animal carvings made by Navajo carvers are for the consumer market.

Origin

The Zuni believe that their village reflects the very structure of the cosmos, the basic shape is oriented around seven points—the four cardinal directions, the zenith (above), the nadir (below), and the center. This orientation is again reflected in the animal fetishes at the core of Zuni belief. Each of the outlying directions is represented by an animal protector. A set of fetishes exists for healing/protective animals while a slightly different group of animals are the hunting guardians (see diagrams below).

The origin of the game-animal hunting fetishes comes from a story. The earth was very wet and hard to navigate when the Zuni people first arrived. The Children of the Sun started a fire which dried the earth, but the hunting animals then terrorized the Zuni people. The Children of the Sun froze many of these animals in their tracks and instructed the survivors to be of help to the Zuni people. This act of magic is the belief that animals of prey charm their quarry into being caught with the breath they exhale from their lungs and heart as well as their teeth and claws. This belief sheds light on the heartline, the inlay often seen on fetishes, an arrow running from the mouth of the animal into the body. The mountain lion

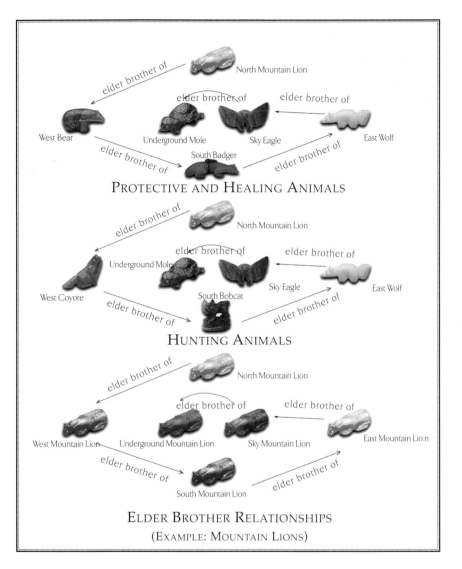

PROTECTIVE AND HEALING ANIMALS

HUNTING ANIMALS

ELDER BROTHER RELATIONSHIPS
(EXAMPLE: MOUNTAIN LIONS)

Each of the outlying directions is represented by an animal protector. A set of fetishes exists for healing/protective animals while a slightly different group of animals are the hunting guardians.

thus became a good hunting fetish for deer or elk; the bear or coyote for hunting mountain sheep; bobcat or wolf for antelope; eagles for rabbit hunts; and moles for small game and underground animals. The hunter says prayers before the hunt and while hunting. He breathes upon and inhales from the fetish. The spirit of the prey further strengthens the power of the fetish.

A type of fetish known as a *concretion* should be mentioned. If a stone or part of a landscape looks like an animal, it is believed the spirit of that animal may reside there. Strangely shaped rocks that have the appearance

An unusual six directions fetish featuring all of the directional animals resting on mole's back. Carved by Jane Quam.

of human organs are believed to be relics of organs of the deities. No manipulation is made of the rock to alter it in any way and this type of fetish is considered to be very powerful.

Carving

Early fetish carvings tended to be very simple and abstract; however, as non-Native Americans became interested in collecting the carvings, they desired more realism in the carvings. So the simple, elegant carvings of Leekya Deyuse in the 1940s evolved into the intricate realism of Dan Quam, Wilfred Cheama, Derrick Kaamasee and the highly stylized Quandelacy carvings. A number of carvers still make the older, simpler style. In fact, one of the great things about fetish collecting is that there is something for everyone when it comes to price, materials, animals, and style.

Bighorn ram carved by Derrick Kaamasee.

Coaxing shapes out of stone, wood, and shell is arduous work. One only needs to look at the hands, especially the thumbnails of a fetish carver to realize how hard and potentially dangerous the carving can be. A fetish carver's hands often show the scars of a slip by a buffing tool. The thumbnails may have grooves cut out of the outside edges. As with most forms of Native American art, techniques have evolved and improved greatly over the years due to the equipment now available. In the past, where files and chisels sufficed, these tools have been supplemented with better saws and finer files, as well as electric grinding and polishing equipment.

Prehistoric and historic fetishes found in the American Southwest were typically made from materials found or traded in the area such as shell, coral, jet, turquoise, and a few other types of stone. In recent years, a broad spectrum of materials have become available from all over the world. In fact, it can be quite a challenge keeping up with the types of stones being used. You will begin to feel like an amateur geologist trying to figure out if a purple stone is charoite or sugilite; if a blue stone is azurite or lapis; or if a pink stone is rhodochrosite or dolomite. In fact, that is part of the fun in contemporary fetish collecting. The same enjoyment is true for the carver as they explore the possibilities of the ever increasing range of materials available for their artwork. The artist finds these materials at the local jewelry supply outlet, trading post, or directly from stone merchants who come to the village.

In carving a fetish from a larger piece of material, a carver may need to saw it into smaller pieces. Artists may envision a particular animal within the raw material and wish to create the piece around the animal

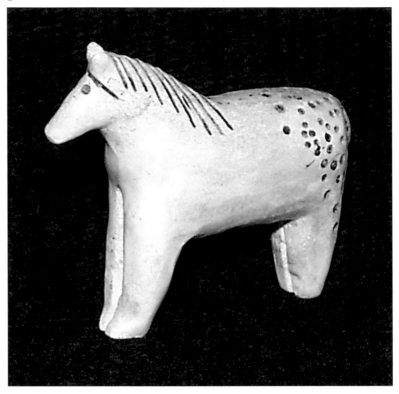

Zuni horse fetish from the 1950s.

they see. They continue to cut down the piece into a rough-finished stage. Then, using a polishing wheel, they smooth and polish the piece into its final form. If a bundle is to be added to the carving, it is tied on at the very end typically using a piece of rawhide to secure an assortment of stones and shells to the animal's back.

Imitation Is Not Always Flattery

As alternative medicines and New Age religions evolved, so did the consumer market for fetishes. Besides wanting beautiful art objects, many non-Native Americans seek the internal power a fetish may contain. This huge popularity in fetishes is a boon to the several hundred fetish carvers at Zuni who rely on carving to make a living.

As those of us in the Indian arts and crafts business witnessed the enormous popularity of Native American handcrafted jewelry in the early 1970s, this demand spawned imitation. Fetish necklaces were the first victims, being caught up in the jewelry boom of the 1970s. Santo Domingo heishi beads were typically used for stringing the fetish animals together. When demand became so great for the heishi that supplies ran short, alternate sources were found. Laborers from the Philippines were used to make the same type of heishi bead using the olivetta shell and sometimes turquoise and coral. Unfortunately, most wholesalers, retailers, and artists, chose to ignore this incursion. Also, instead of using natural materials, block plastic look-alikes of olivetta shell, turquoise, and coral became a common stringing material for the fetish necklaces.

If necessity is the mother of invention, then greed is sometimes its dark and silent partner. Why stop with the stringing materials? The demand for the fetish carvings became so strong that unscrupulous dealers and artists moved to foreign supply sources to meet the demand. Having something made in Mexico or the Phillipines to look like Indian art is not a crime; however, having it made outside of the United States and representing it as Native American handmade is a crime. Those unscrupulous individuals knew the key to success was in having these animals made in other countries at very cheap labor rates and then passing them off at Native American handmade prices. Unfortunately, this greediness has cost the Zuni artists dearly. Every market has a limit to its demand. If the Zuni artists must compete with all of the foreign made fetishes, it leaves less money for supporting their livelihood. The millions of dollars which have flowed overseas in the name of Native American handmade is a travesty to the true Native American artist.

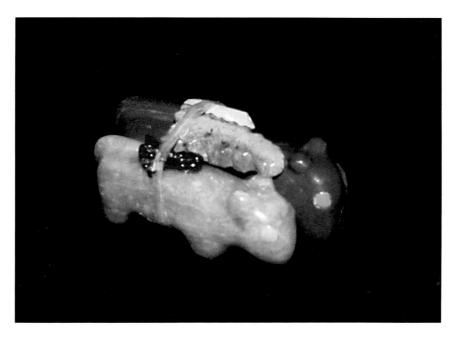

A pair of Scheche mountain lions.

Identifying

- Know the reputation of your artist or dealer. They should be able to tell you the name of the artist and the artist's heritage.

- Learn each individual artist's carving style. Some artists are beginning to sign their fetishes and indicate they are from Zuni, NM. Many more do not sign their fetishes, so look for distinguishing characteristics such as Juana Homer's smiling bears or Thelma Scheche's double coyotes. Your best sources are reputable dealers and sanctioned shows featuring Native American artists such as those sponsored by many fine museums, the Santa Fe Indian Market, the Eight Northern Pueblos show, and the Indian Arts and Crafts Association shows.

Chinese "fetishes."

Additional Resources

Finkelstein, H. (1994). *Zuni fetish carvings*. Decatur, GA: South West Connections.

McManis, K. (1995). *A guide to Zuni fetishes and carvings Vol. I: The animals & their carvers*. Tucson: Treasure Chest Books.

McManis, K. (1998). *A guide to Zuni fetishes and carvings Vol. II: The materials and the carvers*. Tucson: Treasure Chest Books.

Rodee, M. & Ostler, J. (1990). *The fetish carvers of Zuni*. Albuquerque, NM: Maxwell Museum of Anthropology.

A Fetish Carver

Lena Boone (left) and Edna Leki (right).

Tradition—a word that describes the work and attitude of Zuni fetish carver Lena Boone. As a child, she watched great grandfather, Teddy Weahkee, make jewelry and fetish carvings. When she was old enough, she assisted her mother, Edna Leki, with her carvings. Her husband, Rigny Boone, was a fetish carver and she helped him with his carvings. Finally, in 1972, Lena began carving her own standing fetishes and fetish necklaces on a full time basis. Her first pieces were birds for fetish necklaces and other smaller pieces. Later she began to make table or standing fetishes.

Lena focuses on traditional-style fetish carvings. The forms resemble the style of her grandfather but with her own unique perspective. Most of her pieces include a "medicine bundle" on the back of the carving, but she has also done inlaid heartlines on her pieces as well. Lena has been innovative in the use of material and she was one of the first Zuni carvers to begin using non-traditional material such as gold slag.

When carving, Lena looks at the stones or shell and picks out pieces to carve based on the color and hardness. She is one of the few Zuni carvers who uses very hard stones, such as lapis lazuli, and gets a high polish on the carving. Since she is not afraid to use any material, her focus becomes one of color and how she can best use the material to bring her carvings to life and give them character. As Lena is always on the look-out for carving material, she has stone dealers visit her house and she also travels to gem and mineral stores to find more unique stones to carve.

Lena always seems to be busy working, doing five or six shows a year. However, she has also made it a point to educate and train other carvers. She has taught her daughter, Evelyna, and her son, Leland, to carve fetishes. She has also been a supporter of younger carvers, encouraging galleries to handle their work and "showing them the ropes." For Lena, the next generation is important as a continuation of the Zuni ways and traditions. She dislikes the imported "fakes" that are mistaken for Zuni fetishes and Zuni jewelry and the effect that they have on the people in Zuni. She sees the consequences personally as Zunis compete against cheaper, imported versions of their own work.

Lena looks forward to the future and continuing her career of carving. She has won numerous awards at events such as Santa Fe Indian Market and the Gallup Inter-tribal Ceremonial. She is featured in books such as *Fetish Carvers of Zuni* and *A Guide to Zuni Fetishes and Carving, Volumes I and II*. Lena's work can also be found in museums such as San Diego's Museum of Man and the Heard Museum in Phoenix, AZ.

The hands of Lena Boone, fetish carver.

An Artist Looks at Fetishes

Following are questions Pam Phillips posed to the renowned painter Alex Seowtewa, in Zuni, NM, about Native American arts.

How did you see fetishes used as a child?

To the best of my knowledge, since I was a little child in the company of my elders—relatives and other clan members, I have witnessed the real significance of these forms. My patrilineal grandfather was a Rain Priest and I accompanied him many places as his vision was very limited. I witnessed many offerings at sacred places and many old ceremonies that had been handed down. He explained a lot about the ancient rituals and the things under his care. These objects (fetishes) had specific meanings and uses and were accompanied by offerings and prayers.

Did you see fetishes used as an art form in your childhood?

The first art forms I remember the Zuni people using were in jewelry. Both copper and silver were used. The Zuni people learned silversmithing from the Spanish but it was not common before the early 1900s to make jewelry for an income. Previous to that jewelry was made for personal or ceremonial use. I think jewelry was used for income purposes before fetishes. My elders, as my mentors, taught me the interpretations of the fetishes and the use of varied materials. They taught me to remember and that everything comes from within. When I gather the raw materials from the mountains, and woods, and countryside, I can create my own objects. I feel relaxed—no emotional matters intruding—then I can create. The objects come out in all their beauty. As an artist I try to keep good thoughts—positive thoughts. I talk to potters and other artists and when we collect the raw materials, we do it with reverence. It is a gift from the Mother Earth. We give an offering— to give back to her—and to thank her for her presents— the beautiful rocks— the clay—the plants— to give us colors in the dye. You have to feel within yourself relaxed and in touch with Nature.

When you're gathering material, you are doing it with respect. Is that what you're saying?

You only take what you need and use patience so as not to waste. If you look at the ancestors and their dwellings, you'll see they built carefully with the rock and then filled the spaces with little rocks and binding material and it took patience. Their houses still stand and you see

Alex Seowtewa works on an Old Zuni Mission mural.

their walls today—it lasts when you use patience, even with primitive tools. When I need peace and need to meditate, I go to places like this and call upon my relatives to help me. Everyone has a need like this from time to time, to get away and think and ponder the roads in life and to get assistance from those who came before you. Study the past and wonder about the people and how they approached life and their problems. I love to study the art—their drawings and carvings that my father showed me. When I visit an ancient site, I do it properly—with reverence. I don't take it for granted—I make my offering—and I feel the psychological ties. I often go home singing, feeling lighter. I think about Michelangelo or Leonardo da Vinci and other painters and I wonder if maybe someday I'll get to meet them. We could talk and I could find out where they went to get inspiration and help with their work! I draw from my ancestors and ponder the great questions in life and realize I'll never have all the answers. I am just a student—still learning.

Do you think people realize this when they look at Native American art forms—that you draw upon your past—your ancestors—your history and emotions, when you create?

Probably not, but that's why I like to work with young people and young artists and tell them, "Don't get discouraged. What you create comes from within and you need to be passionate about that and talk to people. When you explain to a person looking at your work what the process was and how you create—that's when they look at it in a different light and see the effort and time in a piece of art." Sometimes an artist gets stopped and can't create and is frustrated; or someone copies his idea or style of work. I tell him that is when you know you are an artist. You can stop and think and study what you do and then you re-create your ideas. You get new thoughts and that's how you get better. You have to be challenged. You keep creating and the world can't catch up to you. If someone criticizes your art, you say, "Thank you. You have just helped me." We don't need books to learn art. It comes from within. If no one wants something I have made, I keep it. It gives me perspective on my life.

Are these art forms important today?

Yes, because it's a major employer. Outside of tribal government, the schools, and the hospital, it's the major way for the people to support themselves and their families. It also keeps us as tribal members aware of our past, our history, and our traditions. When I lecture to people outside of my tribe about our arts, I try to explain what some of the symbols mean—to give them an understanding of what's in the art. It's not necessary to go into sensitive areas relating to religion or ceremonies, but just in general terms what some of the meanings are.

Fetishes today—do you see them as a carved art form rather than an actual fetish?

Yes, they are so realistic. They are beautifully carved with a lot of details and sometimes inlayed with other material. The people making them are artists in the use of color and material. It's so real compared to the ancient way.

Is it true that ancient fetishes were found stones and that something in their shape or color suggested to the person what they represented?

Yes, the stones would suggest an animal or purpose and the person would then judge if it would last. Is the material hard or will it crumble away? Can I shape it to a specific use with the tools I have? But they were not nearly as detailed as what you see today.

Do you think Native American arts are as recognized as other art forms?

Not necessarily, but Indian artists are not competitive in the sense that many non-Indian people are with their work. Indian people like to keep things more simple. They don't want to complicate life more than necessary. They aren't interested in playing political games or meeting all the right people. I myself would rather be in the bottom of the barrel than on the top getting all the attention. It makes life too complicated; there are too many demands on you and you don't have time to be creative. I have seen an artist who does beautiful work and is much admired. As the time passes many people recognize it and pretty soon the person can't do it as well. The work doesn't look as good; the detail isn't there. The person has lost the time it takes to do a good job. Sometimes the pressure drives people to seek peace in drink and they end up destroying themselves and their art.

Does misrepresentation and copying of the arts hurt the Native artists?

Yes, since the majority of our people make their living this way. It forces people to leave their homes and move other places to try and find jobs to support their families.

Does this threaten the arts? When I look at Native arts I see a great deal of culture and tradition incorporated into them.

It's interesting how this happens. As an Indian person I have to create and do my arts no matter where I am. Other people can go to school and learn all the technical knowledge on how to do something, but you have to be Indian to really do these arts well. We, as artists, draw on our history, on the ancient ones before us, and on our culture to give us inspiration. Without that insight, that inspiration doesn't come and there is no life in the art.

How do you see yourself as an artist? Is it something you choose or can you give it up?

You can't give it up. No matter what happens, it's part of you. There is no life without art. Whatever else you have to do, you still have your visions. You look at everything from an artist's perspective. You can't help it. You are born with that creativity inside you and it comes out. It is your joy and sorrow and what gives life its meaning. You evolve and grow with it. You have to take risks and do things on your own. It's a constant learning process and I feel blessed to do this.

Katsina Dolls

Georgiana Kennedy Simpson

*Katsin Mana by
Kevin Pochoema.*

As a young girl, I remember my grandmother talking about trips to the Hopi Mesas. She and my grandfather had moved out to Salina Springs, AZ, in the early 1900s. Salina Springs is located in the middle of the Black Mesa/Black Mountain area of the Navajo and Hopi reservations whose northern buttes overlook Kayenta, AZ, and whose southernmost fingers extend out as the Hopi Mesas. They traveled by buckboard to the Mesas to visit their Hopi friends and witnessed the public dances of the katsinam (plural for katsina).

My earliest memory of a Pueblo dance was the Shalako, a ceremony held at Zuni Pueblo in December. I was raised in Gallup, just 40 miles north of Zuni. The twelve foot Shalako figures were most impressive to see as a young girl. Their great height and clacking beaks surrounded by the mystery of a cold winter night struck me with awe, a feeling I have to this day when I consider the beauty and complexity of the various Hopi katsina dances I have been invited to watch in the years since my initial introduction at Zuni.

Navajo artists carve likenesses of the yei'i.

The Hopi religion is so old and complex that any discussion by me, a non-Hopi, would be completely inappropriate. I can, however, discuss the collecting of the carvings in the likeness of the katsinam, dancers representing religious figures. In speaking with various Hopi artists and the Hopi Cultural Office, both terms— katsina dolls or tithu (tihu is the singular form of tithu) are used in reference to the carvings. These are the correct terms rather than *kachina* which has become a blanket term covering the carvings, dancers, and unfortunately the bad imitations of the Hopi carvings. This term has no basis in Hopi since the "ch" phoneme does not exist in their language.

I also want to point out that the Hopi people are not alone in the creation of replicas of their supernatural beings for the collector market. My father remembers selling likenesses of the Zuni Shalako when he ran a store in Zuni from 1943-46. Navajo artists carve likenesses of the *yei'i*. This book focuses on the Hopi carvings, not just because of their broader popularity among collectors of Native American art, but also because of the authenticity problems which have arisen due to their widespread popularity.

Gift to a baby girl.

Origin

Katsina dolls have been made by Hopi men for centuries. Archaeological remains have been found which date back as early as the 1300s. The carvings were, and still are, a gift to Hopi girls and young women. Whether in historical photos or in contemporary Hopi homes, you can see the dolls hanging on walls in the home. The use of the term "doll" in the Anglo sense does not fully explain the importance of these figures in the religious education of a Hopi woman and the blessings they confer upon a child receiving the carving.

These carvings are a part of educating young Hopi females in the roles and importance of the katsinam. The carvings given to babies are a blessing and protection for that child. The simple, flat carvings given to a

Gift to a three year old girl.

baby, popularly referred to as a cradle doll, reflect the development of the person at that particular stage in life. As the young girl grows, the complexity of the carving she receives increases as well. She will have the most complicated carving presented to her as a bride during the Niman ceremony.

In the latter part of the 1800s, ethnographers and other Anglo visitors were invited to witness the Hopi katsina dances. Anglo fascination with the katsina and their representative carvings contributed to a fascination with Hopi culture which remains strong today. A couple of outside factors have contributed to the large variety of carvings we see today. For various reasons, a handful of carvers carve in the simpler style as seen in katsina dolls from one hundred years ago. A combination of collectors' demand for more realistic likenesses of the katsinam and the widespread use of more sophisticated tools have led to carvings with incredible detail.

Contemporary "old" Tithu by artists Clark Tenakhongva, Clifton Lomayaktewa and Manuel Denet Chavarria.

The carving process of the 1970s.

Carving

Every authentic Hopi carving starts with the root of the cottonwood tree. Cottonwood trees are found in riparian areas (wash, stream, and river beds). If you have visited the Hopi mesas, you quickly realize that water is precious in their arid land. Carvers will search far and wide for suitable pieces of cottonwood root. Many buy and trade for pieces brought to them. The cottonwood must be dry before carving as carving with green wood can result in the piece cracking as the wood dries. Many carvers will avoid carving pieces with knots in the wood, although it is not uncommon for an artist to incorporate the knot into the overall concept of the piece. Dried cottonwood root is light and porous, so carvers hope that the piece used does not have an excess of sand ingrained in it, since it can also create problems during the carving.

Ancient carvings were formed using stone knives and sandstone blocks for smoothing. In more recent times, the use of saws, knives, and chisels made further intricacies possible on the carvings. Today, a wide range of tools allows for the most delicate of details to be executed in dolls made by such masters as Brian and Ronald Honyouti, Cecil Calnimptewa, Ros George, and Kevin Pochoema.

An interesting and contributing factor which helped further carvings made completely of wood is the enforcement of the Migratory Bird Act and the protection of endangered species starting in the early 1970s. Up to that time, artists had attached feathers, shells, yarn, and leather, as a reflection of what the actual katsinam were wearing. This Act, along with the greater demand for detail from collectors, resulted in a blossoming of beautiful carvings with great movement and intricacy never before seen.

The katsina on the right is authentic. The one on the left is a fake.

The one change in this process in more recent years is again a market force which places a higher value on a katsina doll carved from one piece of wood.

Pigments originally came from mineral and plant materials found near the mesas. Some contemporary carvers working in the old style use these natural pigments with white kaolin as a base. Later, tempera and casein were the preferred pigments, only to be replaced by acrylic paints. Today, many carvers prefer colored stains which allow the wood to show through the color.

As to the individual representations themselves, it is virtually impossible to own a complete collection of katsina dolls. Although over 400 katsinam have been identified and listed in various publications, the exact number is difficult to pinpoint. The hundreds of figures are not static, as figures come and go with the passage of time. Each of the Hopi villages have representations which are unique to that village. New figures are introduced in the dances while others fade from existence. The best approach in collecting is to understand the individual figures as best you can through thoughtful research and decide which figure or group of figures appeal to you.

Authenticity

The copying of Hopi tihu dolls is not only a threat to the individual artist, but to the Hopi religion as well. Up to this time, the Hopi tribe has

Koshari/Hano clowns are popular subjects for carvings. In this photograph, the clown on the left is authentic, the one on the right is a fake.

Fake katsina.

fought, mostly unsuccessfully, to curb the proliferation of non-Hopi likenesses of their katsinam. As in most copies, the image is lifted without retaining the cultural context. The worst example is the carving of dolls with removable masks. The making of these figures is a direct insult to the careful ritual of the katsina religion.

The vast popularity of the Hopi carvings has led to the proliferation of copies made by non-Hopis. As demand continued to increase, especially with the economic boom in Indian art in the 1970s, a market segment opened for look-alike dolls more cheaply made. The majority of these dolls were made by Navajo carvers employed for the sole purpose of mass production of these dolls. These dolls are rarely mistaken for the artistry of Hopi carvings since they are made quickly of multiple pieces glued together, have fur and feathers glued to them, use cheaper materials, and show little effort towards correct detail.

A more insidious problem has arisen in the 1990s with excellent likenesses of Hopi katsina dolls hand carved in the Orient. Great detail is put into these carvings and, unfortunately for the collector, disreputable dealers sell these at prices comparable to a fine Hopi carving.

Collecting

Navajo carvings.

There are some guidelines that will help you in purchasing katsina dolls.

1. Know the reputation of your artist or dealer. A dealer should be able to tell you the name of the artist. Most fraud takes place because consumers have not taken sufficient time to educate themselves on authentic work. Good carvings require a significant investment, so time is well spent in learning what you like.

2. Every level of style and technical skill exists in katsina carvings. Learn more about what you like by viewing carvings in stores, galleries, and museum collections. Many museum collections only feature the older styles, so look for the more contemporary carvings in retail settings. Many fine museums sponsor shows with some of the top contemporary artists. The Santa Fe Indian Market and Gallup Inter-Tribal Ceremonial are excellent shows for viewing the very best in contemporary Hopi carving.

3. "One piece" carvings command a higher price in today's market. Many of even the finest carvings have carved feathers and items held in the hands that are added to these carvings. Collecting "one piece" carvings is strictly a matter of personal taste.

4. Learn each individual artist's carving style. The great majority of artists know the importance of signing their work, so look for their

Mongwa, Great Horned Owl by Kevin Pochoema.

signatures and hallmarks. Less often, an artist will also put *Hopi* on the bottom of their carving. When not buying directly from the artist, your best sources are reputable dealers and sanctioned shows featuring Native American artists such as those sponsored by many fine museums.

Additional Resources

McManis, K. (1999). *A Guide to collecting Hopi Katsina dolls.* Tucson: Treasure Chest Books.

Secakuku, A.H. (1995). *Following the sun and moon—Hopi Kachina tradition.* Phoenix: The Heard Museum.

Teiwes, H. (1991). *Kachina dolls—The art of Hopi carvers.* Tucson: University of Arizona Press.

Wright, B. (1977). *Hopi Kachinas—The complete guide to collecting.* Flagstaff, AZ: Northland Publishing

A Traditional Hopi Carver

Clark Tenakhongva is an artist squarely planted in the present while maintaining a deep respect for the past. His choice to live on the Hopi reservation keeps him close to the traditional ways and gives his children the best opportunity for knowing their tradition. His love for his heritage is reflected in his carvings which pay respect to katsina dolls of the past.

Clark was born in Keams Canyon, AZ, in 1957 and was raised in the Third Mesa village of Hotevilla. His father is of the Corn and Water clans. His mother is of the Rabbit and Tobacco clans. From the Rabbit clan, Clark draws his distinctive signature, rabbit tracks.

Clark attended school at the Hotevilla Day School and the Hopi Day School at Kykotsmovi. Starting in ninth grade, he attended high school in Winslow, AZ. His budding art talents were encouraged in a high school art class. He drew illustrations for the high school newspaper and yearbook. His work was noticed by the Winslow Mail, the local newspaper, so he began illustrating for them as well.

After graduating from high school, Clark entered the Army in 1975. His enlistment carried him all over the world. As a soldier in the Army Corps of Engineers, he served in the Panama Conflict in 1977 and the Grenada War. He was assigned to Korea, Germany, and Iceland. His favorite stint was in Alaska from 1979 to 1982. He loved the wild beauty of Alaska. Perhaps his marriage to Ann Dora Youvella from Polacca, Az, in 1979 was part of his enjoyment of Alaska. In 1982, they moved to Norman, Oklahoma, where he received an AA in Engineering from Oklahoma State University.

Clark and Ann have four children. Michael is a top-ranked cadet at the Air Force Academy in Colorado Springs. His son, Sam, just finished his first semester at the University of Arizona where he was named to the Dean's List. His younger daughters Carlene and Simana are both fine students at their respective schools.

Several people in his life provided key inspiration in his journey as a Hopi artist. Clark started as a painter, but from the time he was initiated into Katsina Society as a twelve year old, he knew the traditional way for carving a tihu (pronounced tee' hoo). He noticed as he got older that his brother-in-law, Robert Kayquoptewa, was making a living from carving katsina dolls. Eight years ago, while out of a job, he started practicing what he knew best which was painting and making the fancy one piece carvings. He saw artists like Alvin James and Cecil Calnimptewa making enormous amounts of money for their carvings. As much as he was impressed by their artistry, he knew that the intricate sculpture was not the direction he wished to take. In his heart, he preferred the older style.

Clark Tenakhongva.

About fifteen years ago, he saw the old style carvings of Manfred Susunkewa at the Santa Fe Indian Market. Manfred's style made a deep and lasting impression. He knew the old way was truly the direction he wished to head in his own carvings. The final push came from trader, Joe Day. Upon observing the few old style carvings in Clark's home, he encouraged Clark to follow that direction.

In 1994, Clark entered his first show at the Heard Museum. He was surprised and pleased to win a First Place at that show. The same year, he took Best of Division awards at the Museum of Northern Arizona Hopi Show as well as the Santa Fe Indian Market. In subsequent years, he has won awards and increased recognition for his unique style of carving.

His tools are simple. Armed with pocket knives, wood rasps, and files, he carefully shapes his unique forms from the cottonwood root. On very large carvings, he resorts to hoof files used on his horses to shape the wood. His favorite carving is the Butterfly Maiden due to her beautiful colors and intricate headdress. Unlike some other carvers who rely on pre-cut flat boards to carve the tableta, Clark carves the tableta completely from cottonwood.

Butterfly Maiden carved by Clark Tenakhongva.

His paints are unique in the process as well. He abhors the stains being used by so many carvers today. Feeling each piece has a life and energy of its own, the stains suffocate the piece. He prefers starting with a kaolin base, a white, chalky substance found in the area which in water dissolves to a nice whitewash. He constantly experiments with plant and mineral materials to find suitable colors. He has used blueberries to achieve blues and purples. He has travelled to the Morenci copper mine to obtain copper oxide which when crushed and mixed with water creates a beautiful blue as well. A soft lavender comes from rocks found in the Little Painted Desert. Sunflowers provide a nice brown while their seeds can be used for black. Clark laughs saying, "The plant paints can really stink, but they stick really well."

The time spent on his carvings depends on the pressures from his work as the Project Coordinator for the Hopi Coal Project where Clark overseas coal distribution to the Hopi people. When he sits down to carve, he has to move out of what he calls "politics mode" and focus on the carving. It takes a lot of motivation and self-discipline to practice his art. He does find that sitting down to carve seems to "clear the cobwebs" from his mind. He feels rejuvenated when carving.

His current inspiration for carving comes from several directions. He likes viewing the Goldwater collection at the Heard Museum. He also looks at historic photographs noticing the styles carved one hundred years ago. He takes these ideas and melds them into his own original style. He wishes to bring back some of the carvings that are rarely seen today.

Clark feels his carvings are where they are supposed to be. For the future, his only worry as an artist is the fact that diabetes runs in his family. He wonders if his eyesight will carry him and cannot imagine not being able to carve. He looks outside of his artwork as well, hoping that when all of his children have finished school, that he can go back to school himself. He and Ann have put their heart and soul behind supporting their children which is reflected in the success they all demonstrate in their own lives. Every spare dollar is focused on furthering their education.

When speaking about the problem of authenticity brought on by non-Hopi carvings, he made an interesting observation. While fully understanding the impact the non-Hopi carvings have had, he worries that many young Hopi carvers today don't fully understand the pieces they are creating. Because they are not firmly ensconced in traditional ways, they have lost the meaning behind the carvings. He understands that 90% of carvers working today are trying to provide an income for themselves and their families. He believes the Hopi people are going through an era which pulls them between the traditional ways and the forces of the larger marketplace. His stated advice to his own son, Sam, as well as other young carvers is, "If you're going to carve, do it the right way!"

Collecting Authentic Arts & Crafts

Susan Pourian

American Indian art, in all forms, has never been more alive and changing. It continues to be one of the most gratifying and exciting forms to collect. American Indian art combines age-old tradition, innovation and talent. It results in a variety of art forms for all levels of collecting, whether you are beginning with a first-time purchase or have been collecting for a number of years. And, at all levels of collecting, you are helping to support the continuation of the expression and livelihood of American Indian artists.

These art forms, many with centuries-old influences, incorporate a natural spirit with timeless appeal. Whether it is basketry, in which artists are using the techniques and materials their ancestors did thousands of years ago, or silversmithing, which has evolved into classic as well as contemporary wearable art, there is always a place for authentic handmade arts and crafts.

The interest in and appreciation of American Indian arts and crafts has unfortunately resulted in misrepresentations and imports in the market. Becoming an educated buyer and purchasing authentic arts and crafts will help to preserve the integrity and commitment of today's Native American artists. The popularity of American Indian arts and crafts has also brought merchandise into the market that is legitimately represented as "American-Indian inspired"or influenced. This should not be confused with authentic American Indian arts and crafts. This guide should be a helpful aid in either beginning or continuing to collect with confidence. And, becoming an educated buyer is enjoyable, rewarding and exciting!

Which is authentic Santa Clara pottery?
(Answer: The two pieces on the upper right are authentic.)

Tips

Become Educated

1. Read books on areas you are interested in. Learning more about American Indian arts and crafts is often one of the most enjoyable parts of collecting and results in a strong foundation from which you can begin to buy with more confidence. You may also find as you learn more, that your areas of interest may change, with each discovery leading you to another! You may not be aware of the learning process, but it will become evident when you have the knowledge and confidence when making your purchases.

2. Ask Questions! Talk to people who are selling the products. Established and knowledgeable dealers and artists are a great source of information and enjoy sharing it. They can direct you to publications and point out what to look for when purchasing. Many dealers, artists and museums also offer rewarding opportunities through exhibits, presentations and demonstrations. Take advantage of these as you see them made available.

3. Explore trade magazines / publications / organizations. The Indian Arts and Crafts Association has informational brochures on many areas that give a brief history and explanation of the craft, the origins and traditions, and tips on what to look for when buying. Many of its members can provide these to you as well. Currently available are brochures on Basketry, Beadwork, Eskimo Art of Alaska, Fetishes, Heishi, Jewelry, Katsina Dolls, Navajo Weaving, Pueblo Pottery, and Sandpaintings. For your brochures on the area(s) of interest, check with your local dealer or send the request with a self-addressed stamped envelope to

IACA
122 La Veta NE
Albuquerque, NM 87108
505-265-9149
e-mail: iaca@ix.netcom.com
web address: www.iaca.com

The following are also some sources you may find helpful

American Indian Art Magazine
7314 F. Osborn Drive
Scottsdale, AZ 85251
(602) 994-5445
(quarterly magazine)

The Indian Arts and Crafts Board
US Department of the Interior, Room 4004
Washington, DC 20240
(202) 208-3773
(produces a directory of American Indian and
Alaska Native owned/operated arts and crafts businesses
sold by the Government Printing Office)

The Indian Trader
PO Box 1421,
Gallup, NM 87301
(505) 722-6694
(trade newspaper)

Where to Buy

1. Purchase from established dealers and IACA members. Reputable businesses will represent their merchandise accurately and can assure you of your purchase.

2. Ask for a certificate of authenticity or a written record on a business card, letterhead, or receipt. The information should include the item description, materials used, tribal affiliation of the artist, and artist name when possible.

3. Avoid stores with "perpetual" sales or unethical discounting offers. Prices are often inflated and then a flat discount is offered that results in paying close to or sometimes more than a fair retail price.

4. If a deal seems too good to be true, beware!

5. Ask questions—a knowledgeable and helpful staff is a good sign of a reputable business. They can help explain materials and techniques used and guide you on what to look for. When an answer is not known, they have numerous resources and will make the effort to find out. One of the most exciting things about collecting is that the learning process continues for everyone—the novice buyer and the aficionados, the artists, and dealers.
If you feel an item has been misrepresented, allow the person or shop it was purchased from the opportunity to clarify the information—this can clear any misunderstandings.

Keep Records

It is extremely helpful (and very interesting over time!) to keep your receipts and certificates together for the purchases you make. This can be done by simply clipping the receipts and certificates together and placing them in a box or envelope. Many collectors may include a photo and notes or additional information on the artist. Some may even have a journal or album for details and include updated appraisals for their collection. Having the item description, where and when it was purchased, and the purchase price are most important to record. Use whatever method you are comfortable with to record. Keeping records:

a) is a good record of history

b) is helpful if there is a problem or concern with an item, its condition or care

c) helps in time of "the failing memory"

d) is good information for family members who may some day acquire the item(s)

e) is good for insurance purposes—you never know when the emerging artist whose piece you purchased becomes the next highly collectable, award-winning artist.

Know the Law

The Indian Arts and Crafts Act of 1990, PL 101-644, is a truth in advertising law that mandates honest representation of American Indian arts and crafts and sets forth the definitions of such. For a copy of the law, write or call the Indian Arts and Crafts Board, Department of the Interior, MS-4004-MIB, 1849 C Street, NW, Washington, DC 20240, (202) 208-3773. Written complaints concerning misrepresentation of Indian arts and crafts can be addressed to them also.

Common Questions

What are the sources for American Indian art? Isn't it better to purchase directly from the artist?

There are different ways of acquiring American Indian arts and crafts: buying from the artist, shops/galleries, and from special shows/ceremonials. Everyone will collect differently—some only with dealers and some who may add pieces purchased directly from artists. The "best" way overall to collect is to purchase what you like, what fits your budget, and what you can be assured of in purchasing. Many artists establish retail prices for their work and offer dealers a re-sale discount, so the prices you would pay are often the same. While there is a small artist minority who can make their living by selling their work directly, the success of the majority of artists depends on strong relationships with representatives and galleries who market and promote their work.

Where do Indian artists get lapis, for example? That's not traditional is it?

Today artists are using many materials that may or may not be indigenous to their area. Historically, many materials such as shells were traded among tribes. With the arrival of Europeans, trade for other materials such as beads, silver, and gold began. All art evolves, and the term "traditional" may have different interpretations at different periods in history. As peoples have borrowed from each other and over time, traditions have evolved. Today many artists seek out a variety of materials to achieve their expression of art, most often made available by gem/supply stores or through traders who assist in being a source for artists. The evolution of the arts is one of the exciting aspects of buying American Indian arts and crafts.

Which is the best piece of pottery, for example, I should buy? Which katsina doll is my best investment?

When you are buying American Indian arts and crafts you are buying a piece of art—your personal taste and budget will guide you to the right choice. We recommend buying first and foremost because you like a piece. There is good quality work being done today by many artists, in different styles and price ranges. Decide on the style of work you like—subtle detail or very fine detail, traditional or contemporary, or somewhere in between. Some people may collect work by certain artists or artist families; some may collect themes or want particular tribal areas; some may want "name" artists while others enjoy collecting emerging artists' works; and some may collect one or two pieces while still others collect a bit of everything! Collecting and buying Indian arts and crafts is very personal and exciting for many different reasons. For those who choose to invest in the grace and beauty of an object of art, collecting authentic American Indian arts and crafts will continue to be a rewarding experience.

Protection Laws

Andy P. Abeita

As a general rule we, as Native Americans, often find it difficult to express in words our true feelings about our culture or our enduring traditions, our special way of life. We find it even harder at times to express these feelings to the non-Native. Our art work has created a venue for us to share an intricate part of our spirit with the world in such a way that truth and values have been found by many who share our visions of life through our culture and the arts.

As Native American artisans, we have become the storytellers of not only our lives today, but the memories of yesterday, and the promises for tomorrow. Of all the beautiful art work in the United States, none seem to be as appropriate for the telling of the history of North America and its people than those found in the images of Native American arts or crafts: The beautiful patterns of life found in the flowing colors of a Navajo rug; the sparkling micaceous gold tones found in a piece of pueblo pottery, its natural finish, its touch and its beautiful three-dimensional design; the story of the clay itself, being dug up by hand, praying to the creator in giving thanks for this precious gift; mixing water and earth by hand as if it were liquefied gold, then coiling it and shaping it, much like all things that come into the world, a small step at a time, with love and a tender touch. Our ties to this earth and our creator are evident in most all you will see in the images of the cultural arts of the Native American artisan's life.

I am from the Isleta Pueblo tribe. I speak our Tiwa Indian language and participate in most all of our traditional activities. Having lived in our Indian community most all of my life, I have found that we Indian people have a peculiar sense of being about us. Sometimes, we just can't find the words in English to describe the way we feel about today's society, Indian or mainstream. And when we do, it often does not describe the thought very well. People will often look at us as if to say, "I just don't get it." I often hear the elders of my village also say, "The white man, he just don't get it."

Communication always was and always will be the biggest hurdle for mankind to cross. We should be proud, though, for in all our fault with words, there is yet a silver lining. We are, as described in the movie *The Last of the Mohicans*, truly the last of our kind, at least on this particular continent. I think that means a lot. Think about it—how many other cultures on this continent can say that their ancestors walked across these

The Abeita family; Turtle, Roberta and Andy.

lands for thousands of years and have evidence of it, as we do, in layers of ancient walls and drawings and artifacts, as well as ancestral songs that are still sung today about these ancient places?

We have all heard stories about many non-Indian people claiming to be descendants of great warrior chiefs and of Cherokee maidens. Truth is, probably some are. But let's look truth in the face for a minute. If Native Americans are going to survive the perils of today's society, they must take a firm stand. In today's world there are many degrees of what non-Indian society has deemed Indian or Indian-like. I have often heard statements about something having a certain "Indian-ness" to it. This is especially noticeable in the realm of research, public discussions, and general conversations by non-Indians, most notably when used in terms of what Indian art (or should I say, what "Indian-like" art) is. It is in this regard that I speak to you of the importance of protecting Native American arts and crafts.

With the railroad, and the commerce that followed it, coming into the southwestern United States in the 1880s, the Indian communities of New Mexico, Arizona, and even California would see their way of life changed forever.

In 1929, at an All Indian Pueblo Council meeting in Albuquerque, New Mexico, my Great Grandfather, Chairman Pablo Abeita of Isleta Pueblo, said, "We could not ever have imagined what effects this new wind would do to change our lives. Out of nowhere come sprawling trainloads of people and products into Albuquerque and Gallup of things ranging from military cannons and handsome soldiers in fancy uniforms, tons of canned foods, including something they call pineapples and bananas. They bring large crates of Mexican baskets and rugs, that are made as skillfully as our pueblo and Navajo brothers create. Made so well it seems that many people, including our own, now adorn their homes with them. They even bring their women into these desert hills and mountains dressed in white dresses and hats." He goes on to say, "Gentlemen, it is time that we begin to work alongside my friend John Collier from the Interior Department to develop groundwork for the United States to start recognizing our views and concerns about these changing times."

Elders from some of our local Indian communities recall selling pottery, weavings, coin silver and copper jewelry, pinon nuts, roasted corn, and even makeshift bows and arrows to the tourists as they came off the trains in Isleta, Albuquerque, Bernalillo, Santo Domingo, and Santa Fe.

By the turn of the century, there really was little reason for most of the Natives in our communities to create utilitarian products such as pottery, baskets, handwoven belts and clothing, moccasins, or traditional hunting tools such as bows and arrows, spears, or snares. With the onset of commercial metal pots, water containers, and rolls of cloth that could be sewn on a machine, the face of Native society changed forever it seemed, as my Grandfather used to say, "with the speed of thunder."

Natives had not only created these items out of necessity, but for centuries they had also been an important bartering tool. When the times took away the need for utilitarian uses, they also welcomed the continuation of the need to barter. Natives had traded among each other for hundreds of years. In the 1700s, the Spaniards introduced the first trading post (store front) form of commercial bartering after their truce following the Pueblo revolt of 1680. In the 1800s, there were drifting trappers and other hopeful white entrepreneurs who opened shop.

"As early as the 1880s, non-Indian groups, such as the Indian Industries League, The Daughters of the American Revolution, missionary groups, and the Federal Government, began to develop an organized commercial communication line between the Indians on reservations and interested people who wished to put young Indians to work. Between the years of 1897 and 1904, Indian Affairs commissioners reported numerous warnings about the dangers of the growing commercialization of Indian products. These organizations, self-named ambassadors of good will, began promoting the instruction of Indian children on the handmade crafts of their own tribes, trying to maintain the integrity and commercial value of crafts that faced increasing competition from machine made Indian-like articles." (Excerpt from Robert Fay Schrader, *The Indian Arts and Crafts Board*, 1983)

In the 1920s, organizations such as the New Mexico Association on Indian Affairs, The Indian Defense Association, and the American Indian Affairs Committee combined the forces of their organizations to help establish a primary response to the crisis over Pueblo Indians losing much of their land base, as well as prominently affirming support for preserving and fostering Indian arts and crafts. In 1922, the Indian Defense Association was quoted, "Indian arts and crafts represent an ancient economic wealth that still could become important in the Indians' material economy as well as their social and moral economy."

On February 10, 1930, Indian Affairs Commissioner John Collier was able to organize enough support from the U.S. Congress to produce a legislative bill (written twice in nearly identical terms in both the House and Senate) containing all the elements needed to create an Indian Arts and Crafts Board. The board promised to help promote the production and sale of Indian goods and produce criminal penalties for the misrepresentation of Indian arts and crafts.

The project was headed up by John Collier, who had spent many years working in Indian communities on other types of projects. Over the course of several years he had written down comments about how beautiful the arts and crafts were. He could not hide his fascination with what he saw in these fine artists and craftspeople as they created such beautiful work with the most simple of tools.

Mr. Collier was also very familiar with the Indian trading posts. He recognized that, as the times were changing, both traders and Indians needed to develop research, as well as protective measures, to insure the continued commercial successes that had become an important part of their rural existence.

On August 7, 1935, the U.S. Congress created the Federal Indian Arts and Crafts Board Act. The purpose of the Indian Arts and Crafts Board was to assess conditions of many U.S. Indian communities in the arts and crafts sector and to assist in the promotion and economic development of this sector.

The general format of the new regulations read, "It is unlawful to offer or display for sale or sell any good, with or without a Government trademark, in a manner that falsely suggests it is Indian produced, an Indian product, or the product of a particular Indian or Indian tribe or Indian arts and crafts organization, resident within the United States. With fines not to exceed $2,000 or imprisonment of no more than six months in jail, or both."

An elated Collier stated after the final approval, "Through the Indian Arts and Crafts Board Act, the government now was setting out to preserve, enrich, and protect from factory-made imitations the rapidly

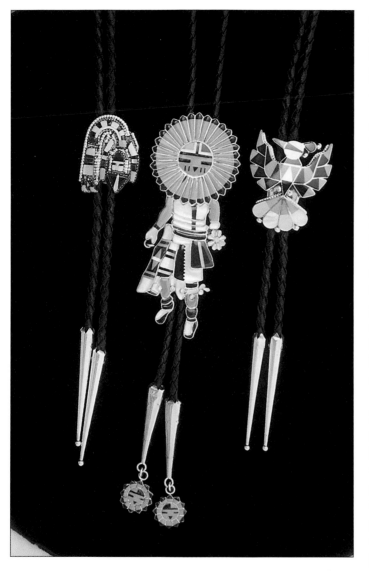

Of these bolos the two on the outside are authentic hand crafted by Native Americans. The one in the center is a fake.

disappearing and unique Indian crafts." And so began the first link in the protection of Native American arts and crafts.

The true heyday for commercial success of Indian products came nearly 40 years later, from the late 1960s through the early 1980s. Although the years between were of great importance in the long-standing promotion of authenticity and quality in Indian handmade goods, tourism and travel created by Route 66 through Indian country brought the important confrontation.

It came the length of Interstate 40 from the eastern border of New Mexico all the way to the western border of Arizona. Billboards read, "Welcome to the Indian Capitol of the World," "Come see the Indians inside!" "Come buy Authentic Indian Jewelry and Curios!" It was a wonderful time for the old Indian trading posts and new entrepreneurs. Tourism in New Mexico and Arizona would never be the same. Still today, the Indians, their homelands, and their arts and crafts are the most popular subjects used in the promotion of tourism in those states.

The success that this tourism brought to the Southwest and Indian communities resulted in an incredible demand for Indian crafts. By the 1970s, production was at a peak. Up until this time, most of the jewelry (primarily Navajo, Zuni, and Hopi) was bought from reservation trading

The bracelet on the left is authentic. The bracelet on the right is a "knockoff."

posts and some production shops in and around Gallup or ordered from individual artisans and their families. Suddenly there were nearly 160 manufacturing shops on record producing Indian jewelry in New Mexico, up 70% from any other time in history. There were 177 retail Indian stores located in Gallup, Farmington, Santa Fe, and Albuquerque, not to mention the gas stations, motels, and roadside gift shops that were carrying "Indian" something or other.

To fill the demand, some businesses began to streamline costs by producing multi-grade imitations to compete in a market that used to consist solely of natural and hand-made products.

Casting shops, commercially stamped silver and gold jewelry parts, and synthetic or simulated stones and shell began to be used. Soon to follow would be the commercial production of import jewelry that would help meet the demand. Thailand, the Philippines, Indonesia, Mexico, and other countries became contributors to the Indian arts and crafts marketplace. Recent industry sources report the growth of imitation products beginning to take over a substantial portion of the international market as well.

With the new wave of production and demand taking a foothold on the scene, there was fierce competition created among the many stores, trading posts, and galleries. Soon the billboards that littered the interstate with promotions of "authentic Indians" and "Indian Jewelry" gave way to "Indian jewelry 50% off!" to be followed by "70% off."

In 1998, New Mexico State Attorney General Tom Udall prompted new regulations to combat misleading statements that might arise from the discount advertising of Indian arts and crafts. Mr. Udall stated, "In New Mexico this type of discount advertising does not necessarily mean that a consumer is getting a better deal from those businesses that offer the discount. In some cases, it may only mean that the business marked their goods up higher to create the illusion of getting a better deal." In the summer session of the New Mexico legislature, the full legislature unanimously passed the proposed regulations. On August 15, 1998, the new discount regulations, 1NMAC2.7 Comparative Price Advertisements and Savings Claims for the Native American Jewelry and Arts and Crafts Retail Industry, became law. The regulations were co-authored by New Mexico Assistant Attorney General Ms. Roberta Joe (Navajo) and New Mexico Assistant Attorney General Mr. William Keller.

Ten states currently have Indian arts and crafts protections/authenticity laws: Alaska, Arizona, California, Colorado, Minnesota, Montana, Nevada, New Mexico, Oklahoma, and South Dakota.

In 1985, with support of New Mexico Senator Pete Dominici, the United States Congress began to address the problem of imported Indian-style jewelry. By 1989, all of the logistical components for creating federal regulations to protect authentic Indian arts and crafts from imports were in place. Mr. James C. Hill was the principal author of the regulations. On September 21, 1990, 19 CFR 134 of the Omnibus Trade and Competitiveness Act of 1988, adopted the amendment 54 CFR 3952, and passed it into law. The new customs regulations read, "All Indian style jewelry and or crafts imported into the U.S. must wear a country of origin mark indelibly marked into the item, either by cutting, die sinking, engraving, stamping or some other equally permanent method."

About the same time the Omnibus bill provisions of the

Examples of fake "look alike" earrings resembling Hopi overlay jewelry.

customs law were being announced, the U.S. Congress, under the leadership of then-Congressman Ben Nighthorse Campbell (Colorado), was also developing a strategy for strengthening the 1935 Indian Arts and Crafts Act. In November of 1990, the U.S. Congress passed The Indian Arts and Crafts Act of 1990, PL 101-644. This particular version, through amendments, brought up-to-date changes to the 1935 act to meet the necessary criteria of today's fast-changing market place.

The 1990 Indian Arts and Crafts Act is essentially a truth in advertising law that states, in part, that it is "unlawful for anyone to offer or display for sale any goods in a manner that falsely suggests it is Indian produced, an Indian product, or the product of a particular Indian tribe or Indian arts and crafts organization within the United States." While this part is a reaffirmation of the 1935 act, the penalty section of the new act is where the most significant changes were made. In the case of a first violation by an individual, the penalty may not be more than $250,000 or imprisonment not more than five years. If the violator is not an individual, the penalty may be not more than $1,000,000 for a first violation. In the case of subsequent violations, an individual may be fined not more than $1,000,000 or imprisoned for not more than fifteen years. If the violator is not an individual, the penalty may not be more than $5,000,000 for subsequent violations.

The Act states that only artists and craftspeople who are enrolled members of federal- or state-recognized Indian tribes fit the criteria to be considered Indian artisans. Additionally, non-enrolled Indians may truthfully describe themselves as being of Indian descent, if in fact they are of Indian ancestry of a particular tribe.

It also includes criminal and civil penalties for either individual or product misrepresentation. A civil action may be instituted by an individual member of an Indian tribe or an Indian tribe on behalf of itself or an Indian arts and crafts organization. The statute authorizes the recovery of triple damages or $1,000 per day of the violation, whichever is greater. The court may award punitive damages, as well as the costs of the suit and a reasonable attorney's fee.

The long-term effects of unfair trade practices in the Indian arts and crafts industry are quite evident today. The overall value for commercial-grade Indian arts and crafts has driven many artisans, whose talented skills would best be devoted to creating new imagery, into mass production instead. There are, however, more artisans than at any other time in history creating magnificent works of art. And in research being done by the Council for Indigenous Arts and Culture, we have found that 90% of the artists and crafts people in New Mexico and Arizona are self-taught, with no formal art training.

In 1979 the Bureau of Indian Affairs (BIA) conducted a national census survey in Native American communities throughout the United States. The results of the study indicated that there was an average of 40%-50% unemployment rate in the major Indian arts and crafts producing tribes, specifically the Zuni, Hopi, Navajo, and many river pueblos of New Mexico.

In 1985, a related study done by the U.S. Department of Commerce indicated that the Indians arts and crafts industry was estimated to be generating about **$700 to $800,000,000 per year**. In another BIA census study taken in 1995, **the unemployment rate in these same tribes was between 60-70%**. In 1997, at an Indian Arts and Crafts Association (IACA) sanctioned meeting held in Albuquerque, NM, a representative from the U.S. Indian Arts and Crafts Board stated to the delegation that the industry was generating well over **$1 billion dollars annually and growing**.

Yet the current industry dollar volume is up 30-40% compared to the years when unemployment was down and production was at its peak. The statistics clearly indicate that the industry is growing, but the unemployment rate in 1999 is higher than any other time in history. In 1995, the Indian Arts and Crafts Association began assisting the tribes in developing a strategy for coping with the situation. Together they are trying to develop long-term solutions to the ongoing problems in the industry.

The primary focus of this collective effort includes:

1) the development of a needs assessment study in each arts and crafts tribal community;

2) the development of internal protections for the arts and crafts sector which will include regulations for licensing agreements between the tribal governments and companies or individuals doing business on the reservation;

3) specific regulations protecting the tribal arts and crafts from misrepresentation on community lands;

4) the development of tribal collective trademarks to be registered with the U.S. Patents Office, and issued to all registered member artists of each tribe to help authenticate their handmade products; and

5) strengthening relationships with outside law enforcement agencies in the development of possible investigations of Indian arts and crafts fraud.

In November, 1998, the Council for Indigenous Arts and Culture conducted a needs assessment study for the Pueblo of Zuni. The results of the study indicated that 88% of the residents surveyed stated that arts and crafts were either a primary or secondary source of income. Furthermore, 60% of the residents travel only within 40 miles of their homes to sell their arts and crafts, and 58% of the residents provide the world market place with all of its Zuni jewelry. The average annual income of 62% of the Zuni community is under $10,000 annually, and about one-third of these community members earn $5,000 or less, with fifty-six percent of the households are headed by a woman with 1 to 3 dependents other than herself. In response to the question "Do you think that import imitations are affecting your current income?" 91% of Zuni residents said "yes."

The Zuni tribe is world famous for its unique and intricate jewelry, as well as fetishes and other beautiful crafts. In theory it produces a multi-million dollar annual commodity for the Indian arts and crafts trade. These statistics clearly show the complex problem of the current commercial market.

Currently several tribes are well on their way to solving many of the complex and ongoing issues surrounding their arts and crafts. However, the most promising development, though, is the recent collaborative effort of various industriy businesses, organizations, and governments in strengthening public awareness of the arts. We must remember the importance of promoting authenticity—to protect, preserve, and promote Native American creations for the benefit of all. As in all things worth saving, in order to understand the problem, one must experience it. In order to find solutions, one must re-educate oneself.

Throughout history, we Native American people have survived many atrocities, often due to our ability to adapt to our environment. When the winds of change come, so too do the designs of life. Thousands of years have not changed our visions of life. The images portrayed in our beautiful arts and crafts are an extension of the gifts of life. In this way we give thanks to the Creator for our lives today, as well as for those of our ancestors in the past. Through the arts we find ourselves telling the story of our people. We offer to the world what we see as normal, to be surrounded by the Creator's presence through our hands and our souls. It is our way. To give.

Recommended General Reading

After Columbus: The Smithsonian Chronicles of the North American Indian, Herman J. Viola. Smithsonian Books. Orion (Crown) Books, New York, NY. Excellent illustrations; mostly by Anglos; good research and overview for readers interested in the Native Americans outside the Southwest.

Beyond Tradition, Jerry and Lois Jacka, Northland Publishing, Flagstaff, AZ. This couple has done so very much for contemporary Native American art. Many people were introduced to their work through Arizona Highways. This book is a sensational documentary of contemporary work by Native American artists with Jerry Jacka's outstanding photography accompanying Lois Jacka's excellent text.

Contemporary Journeys on Ancient Pathways, Art of the Hopi, Jerry and Lois Essary Jacka, 1998, Northland Publishing, Flagstaff, AZ.

Enduring Traditions—Art of the Navajo, Jerry and Lois Jacka, 1994, Northland Publishing, Flagstaff, AZ.

Inventing the Southwest—The Fred Harvey Company and Native American Art, Kathleen L. Howard and Diana F. Pardue, 1996, The Heard Museum, Phoenix, AZ.

The Smithsonian Book of North American Indians Before the Coming of the Europeans, Phillip Kopper, Smithsonian Books, Orion (Crown) Books, New York, NY. Good research of people in the woodlands of the Southeast.

Trading Post Guidebook, Patrick Eddington and Susan Makov, 1995, Northland Publishing Co., Flagstaff, AZ.

Photography Credits

11 Beadwork on leather. Photo by Edda Taylor/Sandra Mendez, courtesy Skystone N' Silver, Hobart, IN.

12 Quillwork on leather. Photo by Edda Taylor/Sandra Mendez, courtesy Skystone N' Silver, Hobart, IN.

13 Bracelet by Mark Chee. Photo by Edda Taylor/Sandra Mendez, courtesy Skystone N' Silver, Hobart, IN.

14 Bracelet by Ira Custer. Photo by Edda Taylor/Sandra Mendez, courtesy Skystone N' Silver, Hobart, IN.

15 Silver bowguard by Robert Kelley. Photo by Edda Taylor/Sandra Mendez, courtesy Skystone N' Silver, Hobart, IN.

17 Hopi necklace by Lawrence Saufkie. Photo by EddaTaylor/Sandra Mendez, courtesy Skystone N' Silver, Hobart, IN.

18 Needlepoint by Rudell & Nancy Laconsello. Photo by Edda Taylor/Sandra Mendez, courtesy Skystone N' Silver, Hobart, IN.

19 Petit point clusterwork by Alice Quam. Photo by Edda Taylor/Sandra Mendez, courtesy Skystone N' Silver, Hobart, IN.

19 Robert Henry bracelet. Photo by Edda Taylor/Sandra Mendez, courtesy Skystone N' Silver, Hobart, IN.

20 Bev Etsitty bolo and Robert Kelley buckle. Photo by Edda Taylor/Sandra Mendez, courtesy Skystone N' Silver, Hobart, IN.

21 Michael Kirk necklace. Photo by Edda Taylor/Sandra Mendez, courtesy Skystone N' Silver, Hobart, IN.

25 Michael Kirk photo by Elizabeth Kirk.

27 Miniature pottery courtesy of King Galleries, Scottsdale, AZ.

28 Coiling method photo by Charles King.

29 Polishing stones photo by Charles King.

30 Pigment mixing photo by Charles King.

30 Pigments in a square photo by Charles King.

31 Mark Tahbo applies pigment, photo by Charles King.

32 Firing series photos by Charles King.

33 Two bowl photos by Charles King.

34 Bowl by Rondina Huma, photo by Charles King.

35 Deep carved vases by LuAnn Tafoya. Photo by Charles King.

36 Fire clouds on Mark Tahbo bowl. Photo by Charles King.

37 Deep carved pieces by Nathan Youngblood, courtesy of King Galleries, Scottsdale, AZ.

37 Butterflies and cross bowl photo by Charles King.

38 Russell Sanchez vase photo by Charles King.

38 Northwest design by Susan Folwell. Photo by Charles King.

39 Susan Folwell olla, courtesy of King Galleries, Scottsdale, AZ.

40 Seedpot by Debra Trujillo-Duwyenie. Photo by Charles King.

41 Mark Tahbo portrait by Charles King.

42 Mark Tahbo's pot photo by Charles King.

43 Priscilla Sagg weaving photo by Georgiana Kennedy Simpson.

43 Calloused finger photo by Georgiana Kennedy Simpson.

44 Weaving tools, personal belongings of Priscilla Sagg & Georgiana Kennedy Simpson. Photo by Georgiana Kennedy Simpson.

44 The process of weaving photo by Georgiana Kennedy Simpson.

45 Eleanor Yazzie corn rug, photo by Georgiana Kennedy Simpson.

46 Carding and spinning tools personal collection of Georgiana Kennedy Simpson. Photo by Georgiana Kennedy Simpson.

47 Heddle and shed stick photo by Georgiana Kennedy Simpson.

48 Opening the shed photo by Georgiana Kennedy Simpson.

49 Is it Mexican or Navajo photo by Georgiana Kennedy Simpson.

49 Mexican selvage photo by Georgiana Kennedy Simpson.

50 Weaving knot photo by Georgiana Kennedy Simpson.

50 Multiple strand selvage photo by Georgiana Kennedy Simpson.

50 Knotted tassel photo by Georgiana Kennedy Simpson.

52 Weaving detail photo by Georgiana Kennedy Simpson.

53 Eleanor Yazzie Stars over the Red Rock rug photo by Georgiana Kennedy Simpson.

54 Eleanor Yazzie's hands photo by Georgiana Kennedy Simpson.

56 Joann Johnson's hands photo by Georgiana Kennedy Simpson.

57 Charlene Juan's basket courtesy of Blue Mountain Trading Post, Blanding UT. Photo by Georgiana Kennedy Simpson.

58 Paiute basket photo by Georgiana Kennedy Simpson.

58 Paiute beaded basket from personal collection of Georgiana Kennedy Simpson. Photo by Georgiana Kennedy Simpson.

59 Heart basket photo by Georgiana Kennedy Simpson.

60 Plaiting technique photo by Georgiana Kennedy Simpson.

61 Hopi wicker plaque & closeup courtesy of Kennedy Gallery, Albuquerque, NM. Photo by Georgiana Kennedy Simpson.

62 Double start coil by Evelyn Cly, courtesy of Twin Rocks Trading Post, Bluff, UT. Photo by Georgiana Kennedy Simpson.

62 Hualapai basket from personal collection of Georgiana Kennedy Simpson. Photo by Georgiana Kennedy Simpson.

63 Split stitch by Juanita Xavier, courtesy of Twin Rocks Trading Post, Bluff, UT. Photo by Georgiana Kennedy Simpson.

63 Pomo single rod from personal collection of Georgiana Kennedy Simpson. Photo by Georgiana Kennedy Simpson.

64 Elsie Holiday tray and closeup courtesy of Twin Rocks Trading Post, Bluff, UT. Photos by Georgiana Kennedy Simpson.

65 Pakistani wedding basket design and closeup photos by Georgiana Kennedy Simpson.

65 Navajo wedding basket & closeup, courtesy Twin Rocks Trading Post, Bluff, UT. Photos by Georgiana Kennedy Simpson.

66 Atsegewi basket & detail from personal collection of Georgiana Kennedy Simpson. Photos by Georgiana Kennedy Simpson.

66 African basket and detail photos by Georgiana Kennedy Simpson.

67 Hupa hat and detail photos by Georgiana Kennedy Simpson.

67 Brazilian basket and closeup photos by Georgiana Kennedy Simpson.

68 Paiute seedbeater from personal collection of Georgiana Kennedy Simpson. Photo by Georgiana Kennedy Simpson.

68 Fishing creel by Donald and Mary Sanipass, from personal collection of Georgiana Kennedy Simpson. Photo by Georgiana Kennedy Simpson.

69 Mono cradle board from personal collection of Georgiana Kennedy Simpson. Photo by Georgiana Kennedy Simpson.

69 Passamaquoddy corn basket from personal collection of Georgiana Kennedy Simpson. Photo by Georgiana Kennedy Simpson.

70 Peter Holiday single rod courtesy of Twin Rocks Trading Post, Bluff, UT. Photo by Georgiana Kennedy Simpson.

70 Hopi carrying basket from personal collection of Georgiana Kennedy Simpson. Photo by Georgiana Kennedy Simpson.

71 Navajo child's basket courtesy of Twin Rocks Trading Post, Bluff, UT. Photo by Georgiana Kennedy Simpson.

73 Joann Johnson photo by Georgiana Kennedy Simpson.

74 Joann Johnson mosaic courtesy of Simpson family private collection. Photo by Georgiana Kennedy Simpson.

75 Leonard Halate dinosaur carving courtesy of Kennedy Gallery, Albuquerque, NM. Photo by Georgiana Kennedy Simpson

76 Navajo horse fetish from the personal collection of Georgiana Kennedy Simpson. Photo by Georgiana Kennedy Simpson.

77 Fetish layout designed by Damian Jim, Navajo artist from Comb Ridge, UT.

78 Jane Quam fetish from the personal collection of Georgiana Kennedy Simpson. Photo by Georgiana Kennedy Simpson.

79 Derrick Kaamasee bighorn courtesy of Twin Rocks Trading Post, Bluff, UT. Photo by Georgiana Kennedy Simpson.

80 Zuni horse fetish from the personal collection of Georgiana Kennedy Simpson. Photo by Georgiana Kennedy Simpson.

81 Sheche mountain lion pair courtesy of Twin Rocks Trading Post, Bluff, UT. Photo by Georgiana Kennedy Simpson.

82 Chinese fetishes. Photo by Georgiana Kennedy Simpson.

83 Lena Boone and Edna Leki photo by Charles King.

84 Lena Boone's hands, photo by Charles King.

86 Alex Seowtewa photo courtesy of Alex Seowtewa.

89 Katsin Mana by Kevin Pochoema, courtesy Kent McManis.

90 Navajo Yei'i carving. Photo by Georgiana Kennedy Simpson.

91 Gift to a baby girl from the Dacia Simpson private collection. Photo by Georgiana Kennedy Simpson.

92 Gift to a three year old from the Dacia Simpson private collection. Photo by Georgiana Kennedy Simpson.

92 "Old" tithu from the personal collection of Georgiana Kennedy Simpson. Photo by Georgiana Kennedy Simpson.

93 Katsina carving process from Kennedy Indian Arts teaching tools, Bluff, UT.

94 Fake and real katsina, photo by Andy P. Abeita.

95 Fake katsina, photo by Andy P. Abeita.

95 Fake and real Koshari/Hano clowns, courtesy Andy P. Abeita.

96 Navajo carvings. Photo by Georgiana Kennedy Simpson.

97 Mongwa by Kevin Pochoema, courtesy Kent McManis.

100 Clark Tenakhongva, photo by Richard Ward, Scottsdale, AZ.

101 Katsina by Clark Tenakhongva, photo by Bruce E. Hilpert, Arizona State Museum.

103 Santa Clara pottery? Photo by Georgiana Kennedy Simpson.

110 Abeita family, photo by David Nufer.

113 Fake and real bolos, photo by Andy P. Abeita.

114 Fake and real bracelets, photo by Andy P. Abeita.

115 Fake earings, photo by Andy P. Abeita.

Index

A

Abeita, Chairman Pablo, 110, 111
Acoma and Laguna pottery, 33, 35, 39
American Indian Affairs Committee, 112
Ancestral songs, 110
Aniline dyes, 69
Apache basketmakers, 56
Apache burden basket makers, 62
Apache weavers, 59
Applique, 15
Azurite, 10, 79

B

Badger fetish, 76
Basketmakers, 55, 56, 57, 68, 69
Baskets and basketry, 7, 23, 55-75, 103, 104
Batten, 43, 44, 47
Beads, 7, 10, 11, 12, 16, 26, 38, 59, 107
Beadwork, 10, 11, 104
Bear claw buckle, 20
Bear fetish, 82
Beeplant, 30, 33
Begay, Bah, 53
Benally, Ella, 53
Benally, Geraldine, 53
Benally, Joe, 54
BIA, 117
Bighorn ram fetish, 79
Bigman, Ida, 73
Bird fetish, 83
Black ware, 31
Boone, Evelyna, 84
Boone, Leland, 84
Boone, Lena, 83
Boone, Lena, 84
Boone, Rigny, 83
Bracelets, 7 13, 14, 19, 114
Bureau of Indian Affairs (BIA), 117
Burntwater weavings, 46
Butterflies, 37, 41, 101
Butterfly Maiden, 100

C

Cahokia Mounds, 8
Calnimptewa, Cecil, 93, 99
Chaco Canyon, 16, 24
Channel inlay, 19
Charoite, 79
Chavarria, Manuel Denet, 92
Cheama family, 75
Cheama, Wilfred, 78
Children of the Sun, 76
Chinese fetishes, 82
Chinle weavings, 46
Chitimacha basketry, 62
Chitimacha heart basket, 59
Chumash weaver, 58
Clay Lady, 27
Cly, Evelyn, 62
Cochiti Pueblo, 76
Coil method, clay, 28 33, 41
Coil, double start, 62
Coil, single rod, 62, 69
Coiling, baskets, 57, 59, 62
    Double start, 62
    Single rod, 62, 69
Coin silver, 13, 14, 111
Collier, John, 111, 112
Communication, 109, 111
    Commercial, 111
Concretion fetish, 77
Copper, 8, 13, 85
    Jewelry, 111
    Leafing, 38
    Oxide, 102
Copper jewelry, 111
Copper leafing, 38
Copper mine, Morenci, 102
Copper oxide, 102
Coral, 8, 10, 19, 21, 79, 81
Cotton, C.N., 45, 52
Cottonwood trees, 55, 93, 100, 101
Council for Indigenous Arts and Culture
    (CIAC), 5, 6, 116, 117
Coushatta baskets, 62

Cradle doll, 92
Crystal Trading Post, 45
Crystal weavings, 46

D

Dance, Shalako, 90
Dancers, 18, 20, 90
Dances, katsinam, 90, 94
Darden, Ann, 59
Day, Joe, 100
Deyuse, Leekya, 78
Diamonds, 7, 10
Dinosaur carvings, 75
Dolomite, 79
Dominici, New Mexico Senator Pete, 115
Dye, rugs, 52, 53
Dyed quills, 12
Dyes, plants and minerals, 7, 45, 46, 58

E

Eagle, Sandra, 58
Eagles, fetish carvings, 77
Earrings, 7, 12, 18, 115
Emeralds, 7
Eskimo art, 104
Eskimo baskets, 59, 62

F

Federal Indian Arts and
    Crafts Board Act, 112
Federal regulations, 115
Fetish carver, 68
Fetish carvings, 75-88
Fetish game-animal hunting, 76
Fetish, Navajo horse, 76
Fetish necklaces, 81, 83
Fetish carvings, Zuni, 82, 84
Fetish, Zuni horse, 80
Fetishes, 75, 76, 77, 78, 79, 80, 81, 83, 84, 85,
    104, 118
Fetishes, ancient, 87
Fetish relationships, 77

Fire clouds, 35, 36, 41
Firing, clay, 27, 29, 31, 34, 35, 41, 42
Fishing creel, 68
Folwell, Susan, 38, 39
Fringe, 49, 50

G

Gardner, Theresa Neptune, 69
Garnets, 10
George, Ros, 93
Gold, 9, 10, 84, 107, 114
Green snail, 10, 20
Greenware, 34

H

Halate, Leonard, 75
Hallmarks, 23, 97
Hand casting, 14
Hand coiled, 34
Hand hammered, 13, 15
Heishi, 16, 17, 38, 80, 81, 104
Hematite, 8, 10
Hill, James C., 115
Holiday, Angelina, 71
Holiday, Elsie, 64, 71
Holiday, Peter, 70, 71
Homer, Juana, 82
Honyouti, Brian and Ronald, 93
Hoof files, 100
Hope Diamond, 8
Hopi, 16, 17, 33, 39, 41, 42, 90, 94, 97, 117
    Artists, 90
    Basket weaving, 72
    Baskets, coiling, 62
    Carrying basket, 70
    Carvers, 98
    Carvings, 90, 93, 95, 96
    Culture, 92
    Girls and young women, 91
    Homes, 91
    Jewelry, 113
    Katsina dances, 90, 92
    Katsina dolls, 91-102
    Men, 91

Overlay jewelry, 115
People, 90, 102
Potters, 34, 37, 41
Religion, 90, 94
Reservation, 89, 99
Tihu dolls, 94
Weavers, 62
Hopi Coal Project, 102
Hopi Cultural Office, 90
Hopi katsina dances, 90, 92
Hopi katsina dolls, 91-102
Hopi Mesas, 89, 90, 93
Hopi overlay jewelry, 115
Hopi religion, 90, 94
Hopi reservation, 89, 99
Hopi tihu dolls, 94
Hopi utility basket, 60
Hopi villages, 94
Hopi weavers, 62
Hopi wicker plaque, 61
Hopi-Tewa potters, 34, 37, 41
    Mark Tahbo, 37
    Rondina Huma, 34
Hopi-Tewa pottery, 35, 39, 40, 42
Horse fetish, 76, 80
Horsehair baskets, 58
Hualapai twined basket, 62
Hualapai weavers, 62
Hubbell, Lorenzo, 45
Hupa hat, 67
Hupa rattle, 69

I

Indian Arts and Crafts Act, 116
Indian Arts and Crafts Association, 5, 6, 26, 82, 104, 117
Indian Arts and Crafts Board, 105, 106, 111, 112, 117
Indian Arts and Crafts Board Act, 112
Indian Defense Association, 112
Inlay, 18, 19, 20, 21, 76, 87
Inlay, channel, 19
Inlay, raised, 20
Isleta Pueblo, 5, 25, 76, 109, 110
Ivory, 8, 10

J

James, Alvin, 99
James, Shirley, 53
Jet, 8, 10, 79
Jewelry, 5, 7, 8, 9, 10, 12, 13, 14, 16, 17, 22, 23, 24, 26, 55, 80, 83, 85, 104, 113, 114, 115, 118
    Hand hammered, 13
    Inlay, 18, 19, 20, 21, 76, 87
    Inlay, channel, 19
    Inlay, raised, 20
    Navajo jewelry, 113
    Necklaces, 7, 12, 16, 17, 21
        Beaded, 12
        Fetish, 80, 83
    Needlepoint, 17, 18
    Petit point, 17, 18, 19
    Pawn jewelry, 9
    Sandcast, 14, 15
Jewelry business, 25
Jewelry classes, 25
Jewelry supply outlet, 79
Jewelry, silver, 55
Jewelry, Zuni, 19, 84
Joe, Ms. Roberta, 115
Johnson, Joann, 73, 74
Juan, Charlene, 57

K

Kaamasee, Derrick, 78, 79
Kabotie, Fred, 16
Kachina dolls, 98
Katsina carver, 68
Katsina dolls, 5, 26, 89-102, 104, 107
Katsina, Mudhead, 20
Katsina religion, 95
Katsina Society, 99
Kayquoptewa, Robert, 99
Keller, William, 115

L

Lapidary, 10, 16
Lapis lazuli, 7, 10, 21, 79, 84, 107

Lazy lines, 51
Leki, Edna, 83
Lippincott, Sally, 45
Lomayaktewa, Clifton, 92

M

Medicine bundle, 83
Meditation, 43
Mesa Verde, 16
Mexican,
    Baskets, 111
    Blankets, 49, 50
    Rugs, 49
    Silversmiths, 13
    Weavings, 44, 48, 49, 50
Migratory Bird Act, 93
Miniature pottery, 27
Mole fetishes, 76, 77, 78
Mono cradle board, 69
Moore, J.B., 45
Moth design, 41
Mother Earth, 70, 85
Mother of pearl, 10, 19
Mountain sheep, 77
Mudhead katsina, 20

N

Navajo, 15, 16, 19, 25, 111, 115, 117
    artists, 13, 64, 90
    basket weaver, 73
    basket weaving, 73
    basketmakers, 71
    basketmaking, 56
    baskets, 62, 72
    blankets, 52
    carvers, 76, 95
    carvings, 96
    ceremonial basket, 65, 66
    child's basket, 71
    culture, 44
    depiction of Mother Earth and Father
        Sky, 70
    fetish, 76
    heartland, 73
    horse fetish, 76

    jewelry, 113
    lifestyle, 44
    loom, 43
    people, 44, 76
    pottery, 40
    reservation, 44, 89
    rugs, 43, 47, 48, 51, 62, 68, 109
    uranium miners, 76
    weavers, 43, 44, 69
    weaving, 45, 46, 51, 52, 53, 104
    wedding basket, 65
Navajo basketmaking, 56
Navajo baskets, 62, 72
Navajo blankets, 52
Navajo horse fetish, 76
Navajo jewelry, 113
Navajo rugs, 43, 47, 48, 51, 62, 68, 109
Navajo weavers, 43, 44, 69
Navajo weaving, 45, 46, 51, 52, 53, 104
Necklaces, 7, 12, 16, 17, 21
    Beaded, 12
    Fetish, 80, 83
Needlepoint, 17, 18
New Mexico Association on Indian
    Affairs, 112
Nez Perce basket weavings, 62
Nickel, 13
Nighthorse Campbell,
    Congressman Ben, 116
Niman ceremony, 92
Northwest Coast designs, 38

O

Olivetta shell, 81
Omnibus Trade and Competitiveness Act
    of 1988, 115
Opal, 10, 21
Overlay, 16, 17, 115

P

Paiute weaving,
    Seedbeater, 68
    Beaded basket, 58
    Feather and bead basket, 58
    Seedbeaters, 69

Paiute weavers, 59
Passamaquoddy corn basket, 69
Pawn jewelry, 9
Pearls, 8, 10
Petit point, 17, 18, 19
Pima weavers, 59
Pinkie callous, 43
Pipestone, 10, 17
Plaiting, 59, 60
Pochoema, Kevin, 89, 93, 97
Pomo baskets, 62, 63
Pomo single rod basket, 63
Pomo weavers, 59
Pottery, 26, 27-42, 104, 109
Pueblo, 40, 44, 55, 76, 110, 111, 112, 117
Pueblo dance, 90
Pueblo loom, 44
Pueblo pottery, 27-42, 104, 109
Pueblo revolt of 1680, 111
Pueblo utility baskets, 59
Pueblo willow baskets, 69

Q

Quam, Alice, 19
Quam, Dan, 78
Quam, Jane, 78
Quandelacy carvings, 78
Quillwork, 12

R

Raised inlay, 20
Red Mesa weavings, 45
Repousse, 14, 15
Rhodochrosite, 79
Rocky Mountain bee plant, 28, 30
Route 66, 113
Rugs, 23, 26, 43-54, 73, 111

S

Sacred beliefs, 7
Sacred places, 85
Sacred mountains, 73

Sacred tree, 24
Sagg, Priscilla, 43, 48, 52
San Ildefonso, 31, 35, 38
Sanchez, Russell, 38
Sandcast, 14, 15
Sandpaintings, 104
Sanipass, Donald and Mary, 68
Santa Clara, 31, 35, 37, 38, 39
Santa Clara potter, 35
Santa Clara pottery, 40, 103
Santo Domingo, 16, 80, 111
Sapphires, 7, 10
Saufkie, Lawrance, 17
Saufkie, Paul, 16
Scheche mountain lions, 81
Scheche, Thelma, 82
Schrader, Robert Fay, 111
Selvage, 47, 48, 49
Seowtewa, Alex, 85-88
Sgraffito, 29
Shalako, 90
Sheep, 9, 45, 46, 53
Sheep fetish, 76
Sheet silver, 15
Shells, 7, 8, 19, 80, 93, 107
Silver, 8, 9, 10, 13, 14, 15, 16, 19, 21,
    55, 85,107, 114
    German, 13
    Hand hammered, 13
    Sandcast, 14, 15
    Sterling, 13, 17
Silversmithing, 10, 13, 15, 16, 85, 103
Silversmiths, 13, 16, 68
Single rod basket, 63, 70, 74
Single rod coil, 62
Single rod foundation coil baskets, 69
Single rod tray, 64
Single rod weaving technique, 64
Six directions fetish, 78
Southwestern Indian baskets, 72
Spiny oyster, 10, 19,
Spirit, artforms and, 103, 109
Spirit, of fetish, 75, 77
Spiritual and mystical figures, 7
Spiritual aspect of gathering the clay, 33
Spiritual force, 27

Sterling silver, 13, 17
Storms pattern, 48, 53
Sugilite, 10, 79
Sunflowers, 102
Supernatural beings, 90
Susunkewa, Manfred, 100

T

Tahbo, Mark, 32, 36, 37, 41, 42
Tansy mustard, 28, 30
Tapestry weave, 47
Teec Nos Pos weavings, 45
Tenakhongva, Carlene and Simana, 99
Tenakhongva, Clark, 92, 99-102
Tihu & tithu, 90, 92, 94, 99
Tohono O'Odham,
    artist, 63
    basketmaking, 56
    baskets, 58, 62
    horsehair basket, 57
Trading posts, 9, 44, 45, 79, 111, 112, 113,
    114, 119
Tufa stone, 14
Turquoise, 7, 8, 10, 17, 20, 79, 81
Twill plaiting, 59
Twills, 47
Twining, 59, 62

U

Udall, Tom, 115

V

Viet Nam, 25

W

Warp, 47, 48, 49, 51, 54, 58, 62
Warp threads, 47, 49, 50
Warp yarn, 44
Washoe weavers, 58
Weft, 47, 48, 49, 50, 51, 58, 62
Weft strands, 62

Whale baleen, 59
Whales, 8
Wide Ruins weavings, 46
Wide Ruins Trading Post, 45

X

Xavier, Juanita, 63

Y

Yazzie, Carnelda, 53
Yazzie, Eleanor, 45, 53, 54
Yazzie, Gabriel, 53
Yei'i, 90
Yeis pattern, 48
Yokuts weavers, 59
Youvella, Ann Dora, 99

Z

Zinc, 13
Zuni, 80, 82, 84, 85, 86, 90, 113, 117
    artists, 81
    beliefs, 76
    carver, 83, 84
    carvers, 76, 84
    community, 118
    fetish carvings, 82, 84
    horse fetish, 80
    jewelry, 19, 118
    needlepoint, 17
    people, 76, 85, 118
    residents, 118

Look for these other Native American titles at your local bookstore or order from:

Book Publishing Co.
P.O. Box 99
Summertown, TN 38483
800-695-2241

Arts & Crafts
of the Cherokee
$9.95

Native American
Crafts Directory
$9.95

Finger Weaving
Indian Braiding
$4.95

How Can One Sell the Air?
Chief Seattle's Vision
$6.95

Blackfoot
Craftworker's Book
$11.95

Native American
Music Directory
$9.95

Please add $2.50 per book for shipping.